Literacy and Language
Handbook

6

Janey Pursglove and **Charlotte Raby**

Series developed by **Ruth Miskin**

OXFORD
UNIVERSITY PRESS

OXFORD
UNIVERSITY PRESS

Great Clarendon Street, Oxford, OX2 6DP,
United Kingdom

Oxford University Press is a department of the University of Oxford.
It furthers the University's objective of excellence in research, scholarship, and education
by publishing worldwide. Oxford is a registered trade mark
of Oxford University Press in the UK and in certain other countries

British Library Cataloguing in Publication Data
Data available

ISBN: 978-0-19-849378-5

13

Paper used in the production of this book is a natural, recyclable product
made from wood grown in sustainable forests. The manufacturing process
conforms to the environmental regulations of the country of origin.

Printed in Great Britain by Ashford Colour Press

Acknowledgements

Cover: Nici Kuehi/Shutterstock

Illustrations by: Anthony Browne; Maria Cirstina; Ross Collins; Mark Draisey;
Lizzie Finlay; Garry Parsons; Korky Paul; Dusan Pavlic; Tony Ross

Design by Q2A

INSPIRATIONAL SUPPORT FOR TEACHERS
For free professional development
videos from leading experts, plus other
resources and free eBooks, please go to
www.oxfordprimary.co.uk

HELPING YOU ENGAGE PARENTS
We have researched the most common concerns
and worries parents have about their children's
literacy and provide answers and support in
www.oxfordowl.co.uk

This site contains advice on how to share
a book, how to pronounce pure sounds,
how to encourage boys' reading, and much
more. We hope you will find the site
useful and recommend it to your parents.

Contents

Introduction

What is Literacy and Language?

Literacy and Language is a complete literacy programme for children in Years 2–6 (Primary 3–7). It is designed to stimulate and challenge children's thinking and create enthusiastic, lifelong readers and writers.

It provides explicit guidance for developing children's reading comprehension and writing composition with support for teaching grammar, vocabulary development, critical thinking and spoken language. It gives you all the support you need to teach outstanding, consistent literacy lessons every day, and to deliver the new National Curriculum confidently.

The core purpose of the programme is to ensure that children, as the National Curriculum aims state:

read easily, fluently and with good understanding

develop the habit of reading widely and often for both pleasure and information

acquire a wide vocabulary

use grammar correctly

appreciate our rich and varied literary heritage

write clearly, accurately and coherently, adapting their language and style in and for a range of contexts, purposes and audiences

use discussion in order to learn; they should be able to elaborate and explain clearly their understanding and ideas

are competent in the arts of speaking and listening, making formal presentations, demonstrating to others and participating in debate

Literacy and Language resources for each year:

an **Anthology** of complete stories, plays, poems and non-fiction texts	a **Pupils' Book** containing writing, grammar, comprehension and vocabulary activities related to the Anthology texts	a **Homework Book** providing further practice and consolidation of grammar points and writing tasks	**Software** with a wide variety of teacher-led activities and teacher support, for use on an interactive whiteboard	a **Handbook** giving clear day-by-day lesson plans for each Unit

Resources

Anthology

Literacy and Language is based on Anthologies of carefully chosen complete stories, plays, poems and non-fiction texts by leading children's authors including Michael Morpurgo, Jeremy Strong, Roger McGough, Geraldine McCaughrean, Jamila Gavin, Ted Hughes and Kaye Umansky.

The range of stories, plays, poems and non-fiction texts in *Literacy and Language* provide an opportunity for children to study texts which are absorbing, challenging and deep enough to dive into, while being accessible to all children.

The children's increasing familiarity with a wide range of stories, plays, poems and non-fiction texts will generate a desire for more reading for pleasure. Wider reading lists are provided for every Unit.

All the texts in the Anthology are complete and are just the right length for children to read during the lesson and to develop reading stamina.

All the fiction and non-fiction texts include rarer vocabulary, which the children explore through Word power activities prior to reading the text.

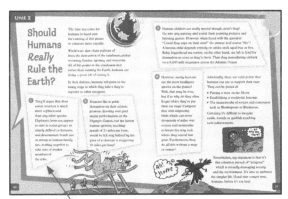

Each non-fiction text is a model of a particular form with a clear purpose, aimed at a specific audience. The high-interest, often humorous non-fiction texts provide further stimulus for reading widely and often.

Pupils' Book

Lively activities in the Pupils' Book develop children's writing, grammar, comprehension and vocabulary skills. The activities are linked to the Anthology texts and help children consolidate and apply what they are learning.

> **Grammar** is taught in context and through writing to make it meaningful for children.

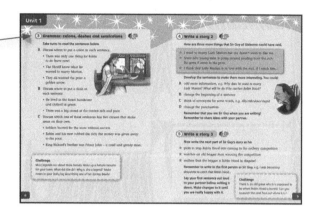

> **Partner work** is embedded in the programme – many of the activities are rooted in discussion, which helps to develop children's spoken English.

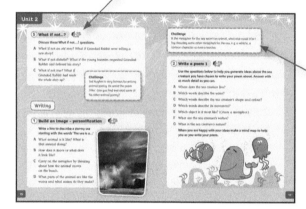

> **'Challenge'** activities are included as extension activities to encourage children to work independently and to extend their wider knowledge.

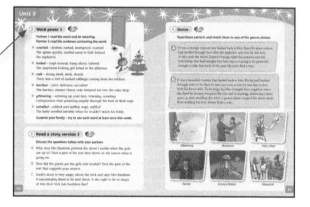

> Each Unit has **activities on 'Power words'** – ambitious words to enhance children's spoken vocabulary and ultimately their vocabulary for writing.

Homework Book

The Homework Book contains weekly activities which allow children to practise and embed the grammar, writing and other language and literacy skills they have learnt in the lessons.

> The activities are accessible and engaging, with age-appropriate glossaries and information boxes to ensure children can work independently at home.

Software

The Software is integral to the programme and is used for whole class teaching. It contains a range of resources to support your teaching.

There are fully illustrated texts, including stories, plays, poems and non-fiction texts from the Anthology, to display and explore as a class.

Audio and video clips are used to introduce drama activities or stimulate discussion.

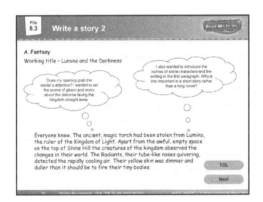

There are **modelled writing scripts** for the teacher to show how a text is built up, including how to 'Think out loud' to show children how to develop ideas.

A **Grammar Bank** gives teachers clear explanations about every aspect of grammar in the new National Curriculum and practice tests for children (see p.9).

Files include:

- video, audio performances of the poems and plays, radio interviews, music and images
- drag and drop language activities
- writing plans which can be printed out for class use
- 'Think out loud' teacher scripts for modelled writing
- 'Power words' for classroom display
- ready-prepared 'Write a story' texts for modelled writing
- editable timetables.

The Software booklet provides more detailed information about the features of the Software.

All this support makes it possible for you to teach an outstanding literacy lesson every day.

Teaching Handbook

Teachers are given comprehensive, structured support from the detailed day-by-day lesson plans in the Teaching Handbook and timetables.

Overview timetables are provided in the Teaching Handbook and as editable files on the Software.

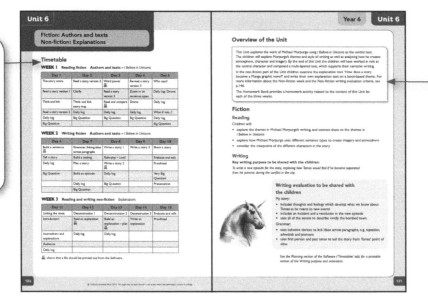

An overview of each Unit includes assessment criteria for reading and writing.

Lesson plans give detailed guidance for each activity.

Activities are clearly matched to the new National Curriculum.

Children write every day, building up ideas, planning, developing longer pieces of writing, then evaluating, editing and proofreading their work.

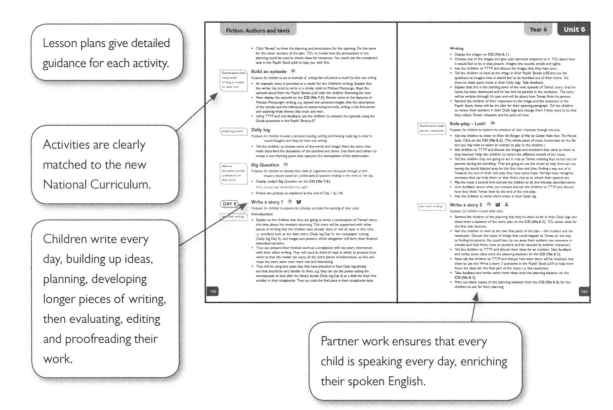

Partner work ensures that every child is speaking every day, enriching their spoken English.

What will children be taught?

Comprehension skills

At the heart of *Literacy and Language* is the enjoyment of and engagement with a variety of texts. Children are encouraged to take their own meaning from each text, becoming independent and critical thinkers. Comprehension activities are designed to help children to infer, summarise, question, clarify, predict and argue a point of view. The children also make connections between texts and their own experiences. The programme approach integrates reading, writing, thinking, and spoken language in all activities, to ensure the daily development of children's comprehension and wider literacy skills.

Grammar

Children are taught the importance of using grammar correctly, so they can communicate clearly and convey their meaning effectively. Comprehensive guidance is provided for teachers, supported by engaging Software, Pupils' Book and Homework Book activities.

Children meet examples of the grammar point they will study in the context of the story, playscript, poem or non-fiction text in the Anthology. The teacher then explains the grammar concept to the children, often using the Software and an activity in the Pupils' Book. Children are also taught the grammatical terms. When the teacher models the writing process the grammar concept is included so that children can see how to use it in their writing. When children do their main writing task they are reminded to include the grammar point as it is listed in the evaluation criteria. Children consolidate their knowledge of the grammar concept through activities in the Homework Book.

Grammar Bank

A Grammar Bank on the Software provides teachers with explanations about every aspect of grammar in the new National Curriculum. It contains a detailed, cross-referenced glossary of grammar terminology with clear examples and 'test yourself' exercises for teachers, with answers included. There are also grammar tests for children that provide practice in the type of questions they will meet in the English Grammar, Punctuation and Spelling Test.

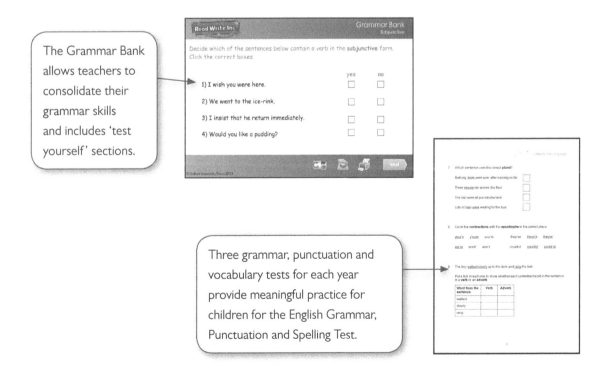

The Grammar Bank allows teachers to consolidate their grammar skills and includes 'test yourself' sections.

Three grammar, punctuation and vocabulary tests for each year provide meaningful practice for children for the English Grammar, Punctuation and Spelling Test.

Writing

Daily writing is at the heart of *Literacy and Language*. Alongside the main, extended writing activities, opportunities are taken every day to create shorter pieces of writing. This allows children to focus on very specific skills, build up their confidence and stamina for writing, and develop their understanding of audience and purpose.

As the new National Curriculum recommends, children are shown the process of writing. Using the resources for modelled writing and 'Thinking out loud', you can show what is involved in being a writer: making choices, alterations and additions while monitoring for sense and meaning. This de-mystifies the writing process for children while demonstrating the 'magic' of creating different effects with language. Writing in action shows children the power of language.

What they read, talk about and see through teacher modelling encourages children to experiment with language to express their thoughts and ideas accurately and independently. Most importantly, daily writing opportunities help children to develop a belief in themselves as writers.

Vocabulary development

The greater the children's vocabulary and the complexity of the language they hear and read, the richer their writing will be. The stories, plays, poems and non-fiction texts in the programme all include ambitious vocabulary. Before children read the texts, they are taught the meanings of more challenging words – both in the context of the story and in real life situations. The teacher and children use the vocabulary throughout the lesson, but also through the week, until the words become familiar. These new words and phrases are displayed and collected from one week to the next, keeping the favourite and most useful words displayed throughout the programme.

Spoken language

The new National Curriculum places huge emphasis upon spoken language. It states, 'The quality of and variety of language that pupils hear and speak are vital for developing their vocabulary, grammar and their understanding for reading and writing.'

Teaching children to articulate their thoughts and ideas out loud and to communicate what they know and understand is critical to the success of *Literacy and Language*. Children are taught to orally rehearse what they will write before putting pen to paper.

Teachers 'Think out loud' to show children what is involved in becoming an effective reader and writer. You can show children how you clarify and modify your understanding of what you read – how you infer and predict; build pictures in your mind; identify what's important; summarise key points; and importantly, persevere when things get tricky. In the same way, children are expected to 'Think out loud' with a partner to check their own understanding so their thinking is made clear to themselves as well as to you.

Literacy and Language uses carefully constructed partner work to make this possible. *Read Write Inc.* partner work is pacey, structured and meaningful – it keeps the children engaged throughout the lesson. Children answer every question with a partner, comment on each other's ideas, clarify each other's thinking, and build upon each other's thoughts and ideas. The teacher listens in carefully, selects children to give feedback and then selects others to build upon what they say. The teacher asks questions to take their thinking further and clears up any misconceptions.

Spelling

Read Write Inc. Spelling covers the National Curriculum spelling requirements and can be used alongside *Literacy and Language*.

How does the programme work?

Literacy and Language comprises six Units of work per year group. The Units are designed to be used over three weeks, but can also be used more flexibly, e.g. over a longer period if necessary as there is ample material and stimulus in the programme to extend tasks.

Whilst all literacy skills are developed throughout the programme, each week has a *particular* focus:

- Week 1 Reading fiction
- Week 2 Writing fiction
- Week 3 Reading and writing non-fiction

Children write every day in their Daily log (notebook) so that writing becomes a habit. They record their thoughts, ideas, and reactions to the text, often as mind maps and story maps – some of which they will draw on for extended writing activities in Weeks 2 and 3.

Grammar activities are woven into the programme on the Software and in the Pupils' Book. In addition, the Homework Book provides an opportunity for children to consolidate and practise their grammar, writing and other literacy skills at home.

Thinking and discussion skills are practised through a daily 'Big Question' which is a philosophical question that children debate so that their spoken language is developed every day.

Week 1: Reading fiction

The story store
The main story (or poem or playscript) the children study in each Unit is introduced via a brief discussion of other texts containing similar themes, some of which will be familiar to most children. Summaries of these texts are provided in the Story store on the Software. This activity helps children to make connections between texts and their own experiences.

Read a story versions 1, 2 and 3
Literacy and Language uses a three layers of text approach to teaching reading and writing. Children are introduced to the text via Story version 1, 2 and 3.

Story version 1 introduces the children to the characters, setting, and plot through about ten sentences – the 'bare bones' of the story. This allows all children to access the basic story straight away. The ending is never revealed at this stage to ensure the children are motivated to want to read the full story.

Story version 2 is a little longer than Story version 1. It gives the children more information about the characters, setting and plot. This shows children how language can be used to change or develop readers' understanding of texts.

Reading Story version 1 and Story version 2 first means that when the full story is revealed in Story version 3, which is in the Anthology, the children can focus all their attention on the subtleties, nuances and their own interpretations of the text. The staged and guided access into the story means that children who need more support are undaunted by a challenging text and can immerse themselves in the world of the story as successfully as the children who need least support.

Week 2: Writing fiction

Build a story 1, 2 and 3
Having explored a text through three layers of meaning, from its simplest level to its most complex, children then see a new text being composed through the planning, oral rehearsing,

drafting and editing stages. The teacher shows how a story is 'built up' via three layers of development (Build a story 1, 2 and 3). Using the pre-prepared resources, you are fully supported in the role of a writer as you model the composition of a text. This modelled writing deepens children's understanding of the writing process and enables them to compose confidently themselves.

Write a story 1, 2 and 3

With your support, the children then mirror the process you have modelled, drafting and revising so that they write ambitiously and accurately as they compose their own extended piece of writing.

The Software provides two versions of a story being written – Write a story 1 and Write a story 2. Through drama activities, teacher modelling and partner work, children build on these story frameworks, adding their own ideas, developing sentences and using them as models for planning their own plots, structures and characters. These prepare children to write the full story – Write a story 3.

Week 3: Reading and writing non-fiction

The fiction and non-fiction texts in each Unit are linked via one of the 'Big Questions' that children debated in the Fiction weeks. Children explore examples of the non-fiction text type, focusing on audience, purpose, form and style through Deconstruction 1, 2 and 3 activities which are designed to reveal the conventions of specific text types. Then they use what they have learnt to plan and draft their own pieces of writing, with an audience in mind, through Write a... 1 and 2 (discussion text/explanation text/instruction text, etc. depending on the text type). A final piece is then written (Write a... 3) presented and evaluated through self and peer assessment.

Core activities

The core activities encourage children to engage fully with the text as they explore character, motivation, settings and themes.

Word power

Powerful, evocative vocabulary is explained and explored before children encounter it in the story, play, poem or non-fiction text. Teachers and children are also encouraged to use the 'Power words' outside the context of the story to ensure they become part of the children's own vocabulary store.

Think and link

Used at different points in the programme, this ensures that children question what they are reading and connect it to their wider reading, own experiences and current understanding of the world.

What if not...?

An opportunity for children to speculate on how a story would change if the writer altered any one aspect of character, plot or setting, developing their awareness of how one is affected by the other, e.g. in *Beauty and the Beast*, we ask 'What if not *a handsome prince*? What if the Beast had turned into *a frog* when Beauty kissed him?'

Build a sentence

Build a sentence is used to build a vivid, engaging description. The starting point is often a single word or a short phrase which is chosen because it is particularly powerful or unusual. The activity is used, with My turn/Your turn, to build up a sentence from a simple fragment to an ambitious, complex sentence that provides children with a model of good writing in microcosm. Teachers model making choices out loud, making changes and improvements, and repeating their sentence to themselves to ensure they can remember it. Sentences can be built up out loud, or written down.

Jump in

The purpose of Jump in is to help children remember vocabulary and phrases from the story. Jump in is used in *Literacy and Language* on subsequent readings of the fiction texts, to help children remember and assimilate the 'Power words' and 'Special phrases'. Once they get to know the story, ask them to join in the reading of the words in bold. Exaggerate particular words and phrases and use actions and facial expressions to help.

Daily logs

Children write in a Daily log (notebook) to:

- record responses to what they have read, thought and talked about
- experiment with vocabulary and text structures
- make notes, mind and story maps, diagrams and plans
- collect and paste related artefacts – tickets, photos, leaflets and drawings from home.

Big Question

A 'Big Question' is asked at the end of Days 1–8 and discussion should take about 10 minutes. These questions explore an idea linked to an aspect of the text covered that day, e.g. after a re-telling of the story of Robin Hood the children debate: Is everyone capable of being a hero? The aim of the Big Question is to develop spoken language and argument skills. Children learn to justify ideas with reasons, negotiate, evaluate and build on the ideas of others, select the appropriate register for effective communication, as well as think in a deeper way about the more abstract issues that come from the text. Children are encouraged to express their opinions and enjoy a context in which there may be no right or wrong answers, just their own carefully considered opinions.

On Day 10 children vote on which Big Question to revisit and explore more fully as a 'Very Big Question' (see p.36). This provides an opportunity for children to develop or revise their opinions. See the Very Big Question organisation below on p.17.

On Day 11 the non-fiction text is introduced through a brief re-examination of one of the Big Questions already discussed in the fiction weeks, helping children to make links between their own ideas and contextualising the new non-fiction text. For example, in Unit 2 children first study poems about animals and the environment and one of the Big Questions is: Which is more powerful the sea or the wind? This is briefly revisited on Day 11 when introducing argument texts which feature non-fiction texts about why animals might rule the Earth instead of humans.

Picture Books in Year 2

The same concepts and structures are used in *Literacy and Language* across Years 2–6. In Year 2, however, the Story store is enhanced by the use of high quality picture books as an introduction to the themes to be explored in the Anthology story, play or poem.

Authors and illustrators include Tony Ross, Anthony Browne, Jeanne Willis and Korky Paul.

Differentiation – guided assistance

It has been assumed that children in the *Literacy and Language* groups will all be fluent readers but not necessarily working at the same comprehension level. Differentiation is achieved by the amount of support pupils need in order to learn something new. The guidance in *Literacy and Language* ensures that children who need least support receive the necessary challenge and that others receive the necessary assistance to understand the texts they read and to write confidently.

The range of teaching and learning strategies embedded within the *Literacy and Language* resources allow you to ensure that all children develop their ability to understand the texts they read, use the spoken word confidently and become accomplished writers.

Teachers support and challenge the children by:

- developing comprehension using the three layers of text approach for reading, allowing access to engaging and challenging texts for all children
- modelling your thought processes in planning for writing and editing using 'Think out loud' and the three layers of text approach for writing
- preparing children for writing using oral rehearsal
- providing differentiated writing frames where necessary
- asking and encouraging children to ask questions, with an emphasis on allowing thinking and talking time
- using partner and small group work developed to a high level to provide peer support and challenge
- encouraging use of the Daily logs to enrich and extend children's thinking, providing a 'safe' place for recording thoughts and ideas and to experiment with short pieces of writing
- using Challenge activities in Years 5 and 6 for class extension work.

Assessment and marking

Assessment is integral to the whole *Literacy and Language* programme. Partner discussion helps teachers assess what and how children are learning throughout the lesson.

The specific focus for both reading and writing is set out at the beginning of each Unit, along with the key purpose and evaluation criteria for children's main writing composition. Each set of partners is provided with a copy of the writing Evaluation criteria (see the Planning section of the Software, and navigate to the 'Timetables' tab for these) at the start of the writing process and this is used as a guide for editing and evaluating their own and their partner's work. The criteria are included in the Pupils' Book for selected Units, and as PowerPoints on the Software, to show that they are integral to the writing process. They also form the basis for the teacher's marking. Teachers are encouraged to mark the children's work thoroughly and give advice on their next steps based upon the Evaluation criteria.

Commenting on Daily logs

Teachers explain that the Daily log is an important part of being a writer – it is to a writer what a sketch book is to an artist. The children know that the logs will not be 'marked' in the same way as their exercise books. Teachers read the children's notes and ideas and respond with thoughtful notes and suggestions. These should be written in pencil, not pen; it will be like a dialogue on paper. Children should be aware that their privacy will be respected and that ideas from their Daily log will not be shared with others without their permission. Although the Daily log is for notes and ideas, it should be stressed that this book is special – it is not a rough book or jotter. Children can leave the front page empty so that, at the end of the year, they can make a contents page for the year's work.

How do you get started?

Book training

Ruth Miskin Training provides a one- or two-day in-school training course or a one-day central training course. A knowledgeable and experienced trainer ensures you can teach the new National Curriculum confidently, using *Literacy and Language*. Please note: *Literacy and Language* should be taught by qualified teachers.

Appoint the *Literacy and Language* leader. Choose a confident and organised teacher to meet the other teachers every week for 20 minutes to discuss one particular aspect of *Literacy and Language*, demonstrate lessons to teachers, observe other teachers, evaluate children's progress and teachers' marking.

Training can be booked at: www.ruthmiskintraining.com

How does the programme fit with Read Write Inc. Phonics?

As soon as children have completed *Read Write Inc. Phonics*, or are reading at NC Level 2a, they are ready to start *Literacy and Language*. Children who finish *Read Write Inc. Phonics* during Year 2 join a Year 2 *Literacy and Language* class. Children who finish in Year 3 join a Year 3 *Literacy and Language* class, and so on. We develop the same teaching strategies and principles used in *Read Write Inc. Phonics*:

Full participation: this is fundamental to *Literacy and Language*. Teachers use 'Think out loud' to show the children how to analyse, plan and organise their ideas. 'My turn/Your turn' is also used to practise key activities and, crucially, partner work ensures that all children participate in the whole lesson.

Positive teaching: children learn at a much faster pace in an assertive and positive climate. They talk more readily in an atmosphere free from anger and tension. Praise for effective partner work is crucial.

Pace: each Unit has been planned to take three weeks. However, teachers might choose to add in extra time for some activities. You may also want to plan time for children to present and publish some of their final compositions.

Purpose: every part of the lesson has a very clear purpose. Please read the explanation behind the core activities on p.12. It is important to make the purpose of each activity transparent and easy to understand using child-friendly language.

Passion: this is a very supportive and detailed programme, which is why it works so well. However, it is the energy, enthusiasm and passion that teachers put into the lessons that bring the teaching and learning to life. Passionate teaching has impact.

Setting up Literacy and Language in your classroom

Timetable 70 minutes for *Literacy and Language* lessons. We also recommend that schools plan for an additional 20 minutes for Storytime every day. Please see the Ruth Miskin Training School Portal for suggested stories and poems to read to children. In the Overview chart on pp.18–19, there are also suggestions for stories and books for wider reading which will link to the themes and genres explored in the Units.

Management signals

Use these signals to ensure teaching is effective and consistent throughout the school.

The 'stop' signal: when all children are engaged in partner work, you need to be able to get their attention quickly and easily without raising your voice. Hold your hand in the air and do not talk whilst it is raised. When children see the signal they should finish what they are saying and raise one hand in response. Do not start talking until everyone has returned the signal and you have lowered your hand.

'My turn/Your turn' signal (MT/YT): there are times when you will need children to copy what you do. *My turn:* touch your chest with your palm when it's your turn. *Your turn:* open your palm to children when it's their turn.

The 'Turn to your partner' signal (TTYP): before you ask a question, tap two fingers together to warn children they will need to turn to their partners to answer. Explain that the 'hands up' system for answering questions will not be used. Ask children to put one hand on their head if they need clarification or have a question to ask.

The 'Perfect partner position': partners should sit side-by-side and shoulder-to-shoulder. (If they face each other the noise level increases.) Number the partners 1 and 2. Children keep the same number for the duration of the whole Unit. See the Planning section of the Software and navigate to the 'Extras' tab for further guidance on choosing partners, and activities to ensure partners work effectively together.

Planning and preparation

All the planning is ready for you to use. However, a thorough understanding of the programme's multi-layered and integrated approach to teaching fiction, non-fiction and grammar is vital. The more prepared you are, the more successful your children will be.

First, gain a thorough overview of the whole Unit. Read the story and non-fiction texts in the Anthology, followed by the teachers' notes in the Handbook, and the activities in the Pupils' Book and Software. You will see how the individual layers unfold; how the reading activities feed into the writing and how the 'Big Questions' weave together the fiction and non-fiction texts. Each activity builds upon the next.

Study the timetable at the beginning of each Unit – it provides an overview of the activities for each day and shows when you need to print out any files from the Software such as evaluation sheets, modelled writing prompts, words for display, etc.

Prepare for your lessons using the teaching notes for the Unit. You could also use and adapt the flexible planning sheets on the Software.

Organising discussion

Setting ground rules for discussion

The ground rules for discussion should inform the whole school policy on teaching and learning so they become fundamental to every lesson in every curriculum area. Children should be taught, explicitly, the rules for working in a group or with a partner and take part in regular evaluations of what makes for effective discussion – see the Planning section of the Software, and navigate to the 'Extras' tab for the Effective discussion poster. Although the rules are similar for all ages, children's responses increase in complexity and sophistication year-by-year.

Display the Effective discussion poster in a prominent position. Praise the children for specific behaviour when partners co-operate successfully.

Short answers
Explain to the children that you will sometimes require a one- or two-word answer to questions – use a finger and thumb to show 'small'. This action tells partners to turn back to you quickly once they have said their answer to their partner.

One, two, three: if there is only one answer to the question, say '*One, two, three,*' and ask children to call out the answer together.

Popcorn: if there are lots of different one-word answers use Popcorn – children call out their answers in the pauses between other answers.

Wave: sweep your arm across the room in a wave. Children call out their answer as your arm sweeps over them.

Longer answers to explain why
Ask a question, then ask partners to TTYP (Turn to your partner). Listen in to different partnerships each time, sometimes building on their ideas. Do not get too involved with one partnership as it is important to observe how well all sets of partners work together – particularly in the early days. Do not give children too long to answer or let the discussion tail off. Importantly, make sure children carry on talking until you raise your hand to stop. It is very disruptive to discussion when children raise their hands/show thumbs or use any other signal to show that they have an answer ready. Select partnerships with helpful contributions to feed back to the group or do this on their behalf.

In-depth answers to consider different viewpoints, challenge claims politely, negotiate an agreement
As above but go backwards and forwards, asking other partnerships to build on the contributions of others.

Very Big Question organisation

For the extended 'Very Big Question' discussion, make sure the children are seated so that they can all see each other. Set aside 20–30 minutes to allow a full discussion. Act as the facilitator and avoid taking over or dominating the discussion. Ensure that all children are allowed to express their points of view and make every attempt to elicit responses from other children to what has been said rather than simply accepting a series of opinions with no real acknowledgement of others' ideas and opinions.

You can vary the way you organise the children, e.g. have a whole group discussion; smaller groups or pairs who discuss and then come together as one large group. Avoid 'jigsawing' as you want the children to develop their ability to sustain and deepen discussions beyond their first responses.

The Big Questions and the Very Big Questions are not just about developing language and social skills. They are vital opportunities for children to explore ways of thinking about and perceiving the world, themselves and others and of universal themes and ideas stimulated by their reading.

Overview chart

Unit	Unit 1	Unit 2	Unit 3	
Main grammar focus for the Unit	Expanded noun phrases Semicolons, colons and dashes Synonyms and antonyms	Punctuation of bullet points Layout devices to structure text	Informal and formal speech and writing, subjunctive Passive voice	
Fiction text/s	*Robin Hood and the Golden Arrow* by Geraldine McCaughrean (A legend)	*Rabbit in Mixer Survives* by Roger McGough (Poetry: the power of imagery)	*Brashem's Tortoise* by Susan Price (A historical story, fiction genres)	
Fiction focus	The legend of Robin Hood and the Golden Arrow has been chosen for the enduring appeal of its central character and its engaging plot. The children will explore the motivations behind characters' actions, use drama to explore parody and complete a number of short pieces of writing culminating in a retelling of the narrative from Sir Guy of Gisborne's point of view.	This Unit explores the power of imagery using 'Rabbit in Mixer Survives' by Roger McGough as its focus. 'Pike' by Ted Hughes, 'The Sea' by James Reeves and 'Fog' by Carl Sandburg provide ample material for exploring metaphor and simile. By the end of the poetry weeks in the Unit children will be able to create their own extended metaphors and have a firm grasp of how a poet creates layered images.	The short story Brashem's Tortoise is set in 1938 and provides an historical setting that is accessible and easily connected to children's own experiences. Children will use this text and extracts from others to explore key features of a variety of fiction genres. They will work in role to explore stock characters and settings and focus on different methods of planning.	
Suggestions for wider reading	Robin Hood: *The Adventures of Robin Hood* – Marcia Williams *Outlaw: the Story of Robin Hood* – Michael Morpurgo *Outlaw: The Legend of Robin Hood* (graphic novel) – Tony Lee and Sam Hart Other Legends: *Arthur High King of Britain* – Michael Morpurgo *Beowulf* Michael Morpurgo *The King Arthur Trilogy* – Rosemary Sutcliff	*Ted Hughes Collected Poems for Children* *100 Years of Poetry for Children* chosen by Michael Harrison, Christopher Stuart-Clark *The Orchard Book of Poems* chosen by Adrian Mitchell *Jabberwocky* – Lewis Carroll	*Ruby Redford Look into My Eyes* – Lauren Child *Ringmaster* – Julia Golding *Goodnight Mister Tom* – Michelle Magorian *Coram Boy* – Jamila Gavin	
Non-fiction text/s	'The Sherwood Bugle' 'Good Day!' 'TV Interview' (Journalistic writing)	'Should humans really rule the Earth?' 'Animals Rule!...but which one?' (Argument)	'Exotic Pets – the Facts and Figures' 'Are you sure you really want one?' 'Protection of Exotic Pets Society' (Formal/impersonal writing)	
Non-fiction focus	Children will study different types of journalistic texts to examine bias and balance, formal and informal writing, building up to the children writing and presenting their own TV news report.	'Should humans really rule the Earth?' is a balanced argument text that explores whether or not animals might make a better job of looking after the planet than humans. 'Animals Rule!' is a series of persuasive paragraphs, which put across five animals' point of view as to why their species should rule the Earth. Children study how to create balanced arguments as well as exploring how to organise a persuasive paragraph.	Children will study examples of impersonal/formal writing, including work on the passive/ active voice in sentences, present tense and complex sentences. They will write short examples of formal/ impersonal texts. Finally, children will plan and enact a short role-play based on an encounter between a customs officer and someone they suspect is trying to smuggle an exotic animal for the pet market.	

	Unit 4	Unit 5	Unit 6
	Formal and informal vocabulary	Hyphens to avoid ambiguity	Linking ideas across paragraphs using a wide range of cohesive devices
	Gone Away! by Lou Kuenzler (A story with flashbacks)	*The Elephant in the Room* by Lou Kuenzler (A playscript, narratives and plays)	*I Believe in Unicorns* by Michael Morpurgo (Authors and texts)
	Lou Kuenzler's story Gone Away! uses economical but evocative language and flashbacks to explore friendship, loss and guilt. Children will experiment with these techniques in their own writing. Please note that Gone Away! explores the potentially sensitive subject of bereavement and this should be taken into account in particular teaching circumstances.	The playscript The Elephant in the Room is about a child-carer. Children will study the plot, characters and dramatic conventions, and elements of performance are included. Children will build a character and explore the stages of development of a script, then go on to write an extra scene for the play.	This Unit explores the work of Michael Morpurgo using I Believe in Unicorns as the central text. The children will study Morpurgo's themes and style of writing as well as analysing how he creates atmosphere, character and imagery. Children will work in role as the central character and compose a multi-layered text, which supports their narrative writing.
	Stories with Flashbacks: *Tom's Midnight Garden* – Philippa Pearce Stories about Friendship: *Holes* – Louis Sachar *Wonder* – RJ Palacio *Daisy Star, Ooh La La!* – Cathy Cassidy *Stargirl* – Jerry Spinelli *Stig of the Dump* – Clive King	*Zelah Green Queen of Clean* – Vanessa Curtis *Shine* – Kate Maryon *The Hunger Games* – Suzanne Collins	*Singing for Mrs Pettigrew, War Horse, Private Peaceful* – Michael Morpurgo *The Silver Sword* – Ian Serraillier *Carrie's War* – Nina Bawden *When Hitler Stole Pink Rabbit* – Judith Kerr *Just Henry* – Michelle Magorian
	'Alexander Selkirk Biography' (Biography and autobiography)	'Make memory lapses a thing to forget!' 'Memoraid' (Persuasive texts)	'How does a story become a Manga graphic novel?' (Explanations)
	Biographical and autobiographical reading and writing will be explored. Children will use a variety of resources to research a biographical subject. They will create a PowerPoint presentation of a biography and participate in peer evaluations. They will go on to write their own autobiographies.	Children will study persuasive texts, looking at biased articles, advertorials and adverts. Children will write a scripted presentation and use it to persuade the class to vote either for or against the use of a brain boosting memory aid in schools.	Children will study the non-fiction explanation text 'How does a story become a Manga graphic novel?' and write their own explanation on a book-based theme using a range of Internet sources.

Fiction: Legends
Non-fiction: Journalistic Writing

Timetable

WEEK 1 **Reading fiction** *Robin Hood and the Golden Arrow*

Day 1	Day 2	Day 3	Day 4	Day 5
The story store	Word power 1 🖶	Word power 2 🖶	Re-read a story version 3	Showing and telling
Read a story version 1	Context	Special phrases 🖶	Grammar: expanded noun phrases	Dramatic reconstruction
Think and link 1 🖶	Read a story version 3	Read a story version 3	What if not...? 🖶	Daily log
Read a story version 2	Daily log	What should I do?	What do I want? How do I get it?	Big Question
Daily log	Big Question	Daily log	Daily log	
Big Question		Big Question	Big Question	

WEEK 2 **Writing fiction** *Robin Hood and the Golden Arrow*

Day 6	Day 7	Day 8	Day 9	Day 10
Build a setting	Grammar: colons, dashes and semicolons	Write a story 1	Write a story 3	Share a story
Contexts	Build a story 1	Write a story 2		Evaluate and edit
Daily log	Build a story 2	Daily log		Proofread
Big Question	Build a story 3 🖶	Big Question		Very Big Question
	Daily Log			
	Big Question			

WEEK 3 **Reading and writing non-fiction** Journalistic Writing

Day 11	Day 12	Day 13	Day 14	Day 15
Introduction 🖶	Deconstruction 1 🖶	Deconstruction 2	Deconstruction 3	TV news presentations 🖶
Word power 🖶	Write a news report 1	Write a news report 2	Write a news report 3	Evaluate and edit
Journalistic texts	Daily log	Daily log	Proofread	
Five Ws 🖶			Daily log	
Daily log				

🖶: shows that a file should be printed out from the Software.

Overview of the Unit

The legend of *Robin Hood and the Golden Arrow* has been chosen for the enduring appeal of its central character and its engaging plot. This lightly ironic version by Geraldine McCaughrean combines vivid imagery and powerful vocabulary to create a humorous but poignant tale. The children will explore the motivations behind characters' actions, use drama to explore parody and complete a number of short pieces of writing culminating in a retelling of the narrative from Sir Guy of Gisborne's point of view.

The linked non-fiction work introduces different types of journalistic texts to examine bias and balance, formal and informal writing. The activities build up to the children writing and presenting their own TV news report. For more information about the Non-fiction week and the Non-fiction writing evaluation criteria, see p.37.

The Homework Book provides a homework activity related to the content of this Unit for each of the three weeks.

Fiction

Reading

Children will:

- understand that legends can tell us useful and interesting things about the past
- make connections between *Robin Hood*, other legends they have read and their own experiences
- identify how the author helps the reader to visualise the story by using vivid imagery, including metaphor
- understand what the characters' actions might reveal about their motivations.

Writing

Key writing purpose to be shared with the children:

To retell the story of Robin Hood in role as Sir Guy of Gisborne.

Writing evaluation to be shared with the children

My new episode:

- retells the story in role as Sir Guy of Gisborne
- makes Robin Hood appear in a bad light by using negative descriptions (to show Guy of Gisborne's point of view)
- describes Sir Guy's motivations by *showing* the reader how he feels about Robin Hood rather than *telling*.

Grammar:

- includes expanded noun phrases to create ambitious descriptions, e.g. *that worthless, thieving peasant*.

See the Planning section of the Software ('Timetables' tab) for a printable version of the Writing purpose and evaluation.

Fiction: Legends
Robin Hood and the Golden Arrow
by Geraldine McCaughrean

READING FICTION

Resources

 Pupils' Book, pp.4–11

Anthology, pp.4–17

CD on interactive whiteboard (Unit 1)

GB Grammar Bank on CD

HB Homework Book, pp.4–7

DAY 1

Curriculum link:
identifying and discussing themes and conventions, making comparisons within and across stories

The story store

Purpose: for children to develop their existing knowledge of familiar features of legends

- Remind the children that a legend is a story about a person, a place or an event that we believe to have been true (although we can't be sure). However over many years, storytellers have added to the story to make it more exciting and so whatever truth there was can be hard to find.
- Tell the children that just like other traditional tales, such as fairy stories, myths and fables, legends were not written down for many years, so as people told each other the legend some things would be changed or forgotten altogether. That is why lots of different versions of the same legends exist.
- Explain that many legends tell us about how people lived hundreds of years ago and the things that were important to them.
- Use the **CD (file 1.1)** to display summaries of the legends of *Sir Gawain and the Green Knight* and *William Tell* to show children some key features of legends. Read them to the children.
- Tell the children they are now going to hear the bare bones of a very famous legend that has similar features to parts of the *William Tell* and the *Sir Gawain and the Green Knight* legends and we are going to call it Story version 1. It is one of many tales about the daring deeds of a cheeky but brave outlaw who stands up to a cruel ruler.

read legends

Read a story version 1

Purpose: for children to become familiar with Story version 1, the bare bones of the legend of Robin Hood and the Golden Arrow

- Read Story version 1 aloud all the way through to the children. (Do not reveal any surprises or the ending of the final story.) Note that the PowerPoint files open in a view which allows them to be edited. To take advantage of the full functionality of the files you should view them in Slide Show mode. Press F5 on the keyboard or select 'Slide Show' then 'View Show' from the PowerPoint toolbar.

Story version 1
1. A cruel prince and his men keep money and other riches for themselves and starve the poor.
2. They take land away from a young man. He makes a secret home in a forest.
3. He robs from the rich and gives it away to the poor.
4. The mean Prince sends his soldiers to search for this puzzling robber.
5. The young robber is known as the best archer in the land.
6. Someone makes a plan to trap the young outlaw.
7. An archery competition is part of the plan.
8. The young man puts himself at risk to try to win the prize.
9. The competition begins.
10. Someone is punished.

- Use MT/YT (My turn/Your turn) and TTYP (Turn to your partner) for each point – you will need to break down the longer points. Use exaggerated intonation and emphasis where appropriate. This is to help the children to 'hold' the basic story in their heads.

Think and link 1

Curriculum link:
making comparisons

Purpose: for children to make links and connections with other stories and their own experiences

- Display Story version 1 on the **CD (file 1.2)**. Talk through each section with the children; show how you link what you know about the story and characters so far with your own experiences and other stories. TOL (Think out loud) using your own words or print the script from the **CD (file 1.3)**.
- Use TTYP and feedback to allow children to articulate and share ideas/connections and for you to paraphrase, clarify and extend their thoughts and ideas.

Read a story version 2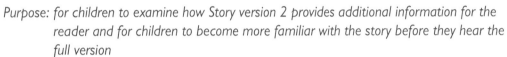

predicting; identifying how language, structure, and presentation contribute to meaning

Purpose: for children to examine how Story version 2 provides additional information for the reader and for children to become more familiar with the story before they hear the full version

- Read Story version 2 to the children.
  Story version 2
  1. A callous prince and his barons keep money and other riches for themselves and make the poor pay taxes until they starve.
  2. One of those barons, Sir Guy of Gisborne, steals land away from a young man called Robin of Locksley.
  3. Robin makes a hideaway home in a forest. Others join him to live in the forest.
  4. He becomes a mysterious hero as he pinches from the rich and gives it away to the poor and starving.
  5. Heartless Prince John sends his soldiers to hunt everywhere for this shadowy figure.
  6. Robin is known as an expert with a bow and arrow. He is the finest archer in all the land.
  7. The Sheriff and Sir Guy are desperate to catch the young outlaw and they make a plan to trap him into coming to Sir Guy's castle.
  8. Robin hears about an archery competition. Sir Guy hopes that the man of the forest will not be able to resist showing off his skills.
  9. Robin puts himself in jeopardy in order to win the Prince's prize, a golden arrow.
  10. Rich and poor flock to the castle. The archery contest is launched!
  11. Someone is in for a great surprise and someone is going to be punished...

- Re-read it, stopping after each section to ask the children if there are any words that tell them more about the people and the story. TTYP and feed back.
- Now display this version on the **CD (file 1.4)**. Click 'Highlights' to show highlighted additional information:
  - We know characters' names – *Prince John, Sir Guy of Gisborne, Robin of Locksley*
  - Addition of the fact that *the poor are made to pay taxes to the Prince.*
  - Addition of the fact that *others join Robin to live in the forest.*
  - Addition of adjectives, e.g. *mysterious* and *shadowy* to describe Robin of Locksley.
  - We know that the Prince and Sir Guy are *desperate* to catch Robin
  - We know that the prize for the archery competition is a *golden arrow.*
  - People came to the castle and someone will be surprised.
- TOL and use TTYP to share how this extra information changes the pictures in our minds as we hear the story. Collect feedback.

Fiction: Legends

Curriculum link: making comparisons, identifying themes

Daily log

Purpose: for children to be introduced to the process of keeping a personal log of notes, thoughts and ideas, collected from their reading and discussions, to use in their own writing

- Explain that many people make notes of their thoughts about things they see, hear, read and think about. Lots of writers do this and use the ideas in their own writing. They might collect cuttings and pictures, draw mind maps and diagrams, invent their own symbols as well as writing in prose. Explain that the children are going to collect their thoughts and ideas in a Daily log.
- Ask the children to TTYP to discuss which parts or features of the *William Tell, Sir Gawain and the Green Knight* and the *Robin Hood* legends are similar, e.g. Robin and the Green Knight are both dressed in green, William Tell and Robin are both the best archers in their lands, etc. Ask them to record their thoughts in their Daily log.

Big Question ⓒⒹ

effective discussion; provide justifications for their views

Purpose: for children to develop their skills of argument and discussion through a mini enquiry session based on a philosophical question relating to the work of the day

- Display today's Big Question on the **CD (file 1.5)**:

  Is stealing always wrong?

- Ask the children to TTYP to discuss. Collect feedback from partners and scribe responses. Tell them that each day's Big Question and their thoughts written on paper will be put in a safe place until the end of week 2. They will then vote on which question to discuss more deeply. See Introduction for further notes (p.13).

DAY 2

Word power 1 Synonyms and antonyms ⓒⒹ

exploring the meaning of words in context

Purpose: for children to increase their knowledge and application of synonyms and to examine how writers use language for effect

> cruel   mean   callous   heartless   takes   steals   robs   pinches
> puzzling   mysterious   shadowy   at risk   in jeopardy   begins   is launched

- Tell the children that there are different words in Story version 2 that mean the same thing as *cruel* and *mean* in Story version 1. Tell them that these *synonyms* can show just how cruel someone is.
- Display Story version 1 and Story version 2 on the **CD (file 2.1)** and click 'Synonyms' to identify the synonyms – *cruel/mean/callous/heartless* (navigate to screen 2 to see the second pair).
- Identify other examples of synonymous words highlighted: *takes/steals/robs/ pinches   puzzling/mysterious/shadowy   at risk/in jeopardy   begins/is launched*
- TOL and use TTYP to share an example of how some of these words change the pictures in our minds. TTYP, asking the children to discuss other examples.
- Print all of the words and their synonyms from the **CD (file 2.2)** and display them on your Power word wall.
- Remind the children that an antonym is a word that means the opposite of another word. Use MT/YT to say 'antonym'.
- Write these words on the board or a flip chart: *cruel   takes   puzzling   begins* and ask the children to TTYP to think of an antonym for each of these words.
- Choose sets of partners to share their antonyms. Write their suggestions on the board, clarifying and correcting where necessary. You may wish to write the words on card and add to your word wall. Try to use some of these words during the day where appropriate, pointing at them on your word wall as you say them.

- Find opportunities to use the words yourself during the day, e.g. "I saw some *barbaric* behaviour in the playground – it must be *eliminated*!" and encourage the children to use them in their everyday conversation.
- Encourage the children to use the words at home with friends and family so that they become embedded in their own spoken (and eventually, written) vocabulary.
- Print all of these words and their definitions from the **CD (file 3.2)** and display them on your Word wall.

Curriculum link: exploring the meaning of words in context

Special phrases

Purpose: for children to become familiar with special phrases particular to the story

> *The Normans fed richly off the fat of the land.*
>
> *Their very existence burned like a green gleam in the imagination.*
>
> *...restored to youth.*
>
> *The telling of his thousand daring deeds warmed them...*
>
> *Robin was the green promise that spring always returns.*

- Display the **CD (file 3.3)** to show the special phrases from the story. These can be printed off from the **CD (file 3.4)** for your word wall.
- Explain that you have chosen these because they are phrases that we don't use in our everyday talk and also because they are linked to important moments in the story. Read the phrases out loud with enjoyment, adding expression and intonation to add further meaning to the phrase.
- Now TOL as you draw attention to particular features of some of the phrases that you like, e.g. rhyme – *green gleam*; alliteration – *daring deeds*; simile – *burned like a green gleam*; metaphors – *the green promise that spring always returns*; rhythm of the words together – *the fat of the land*.
- Now ask the children to TTYP to read the special phrases and their meanings given in the Special phrases activity in the Pupils' Book p.5. Ask them to each choose their favourite special phrase and to explain to their partner what they like about it. Choose some partners to feed back.

checking that the story makes sense to them

Read a story version 3

Purpose: for children to gain a deeper understanding of the story they have heard and to see the text for the first time

- Let the children follow their own copy of the text in their Anthology p.4 as you re-read the full version of the story aloud with great enthusiasm. Put special emphasis on the Power words in bold and stop at the Special phrases so that the children can "jump in". See Introduction for further notes (p.13).
- Now ask the children to read their copy of the story with their partners, alternating sections. Encourage them to read the words and phrases in bold with great expression! Explain that you will be listening in.

identifying key details

What should I do?

Purpose: for children to understand how writers use dilemmas and responses in narrative to subvert or meet readers' expectations

- Tell the children that in this legend, like all stories, characters find themselves faced with a problem or dilemma and they take action to resolve each dilemma.
- Now explain that sometimes characters might not respond to dilemmas in the way we expect them to. Display the **CD (file 3.5)** to show the dilemmas grid.

Use drag and drop to choose the action Robin actually took in the story for Dilemma A. Briefly TOL about the consequences of the action taken. Bring the children into the TOL.

- Ask the children to TTYP to discuss the most likely and the least likely alternative option from those provided. Collect feedback and use drag and drop to complete the grid, clarifying and expanding ideas as necessary.

Daily log

Curriculum link: discussing their understanding of words in context

Purpose: for children to keep a personal reading, writing and thinking log in order to record thoughts and ideas for their own writing

- Ask the children to decide on their favourite Word power words and/or Special phrases from the story and explain why they like them. Ask them to TTYP to share and then record them in their Daily log.

Big Question ⓒⒹ

effective discussion; provide justifications for their views

Purpose: for children to develop their skills of argument and discussion through a mini enquiry session based on a philosophical question relating to the work of the day

- Display today's Big Question on the **CD (file 3.6)**:

  Is it right for some people to be richer than others?

- Follow the process as explained at the end of Day 1 (p.24).

DAY 4

Re-read a story version 3 Ⓐ

read silently

Purpose: for children to deepen their understanding of a story by increasing familiarity with the text

- Ask the children to read the whole story silently from the Anthology p.4. Tell them that they can stop to record any thoughts, ideas, questions and favourite bits in their Daily log as they read the text. Explain that it is more important for them to think about what they are reading than to finish first and, as they already know the story, it doesn't matter if they don't finish this time.

Grammar: expanded noun phrases Ⓐ ⓒⒹ ⓟⒷ

Year 6 Grammar expanded noun phrases to convey complicated information concisely

Purpose: for children to revise and develop their ability to recognise and create expanded noun phrases to convey information concisely

- Tell the children that the writer of the story *Robin Hood and the Golden Arrow*, Geraldine McCaughrean, is very skilful at including lots of information to create interesting sentences that help us to create detailed pictures in our minds of characters, events and settings.
- Explain that she builds words around a simple *noun*, to give us extra, important information. Display **CD (file 4.1)** to show the noun 'man' and say that this is a common noun and could be referring to any man.
- Tell them that the writer added an adjective before the noun. This has created a noun phrase – a group of more than one word including the noun. Click 'Reveal' to show the noun phrase and then read the explanatory think bubble.
- Say that the writer has expanded the noun phrase further by adding some more adjectives after the noun. Click 'Next' to show the expanded noun phrase and ask the children to identify the adjectives by saying them aloud chorally. Click 'Highlight' to highlight the adjectives for verification.

- Explain that the writer could have placed *all* of the adjectives *before* the noun or *all* of them *after* the noun. Click 'Next' to show the two alternative versions. Read them out chorally with the children.
- Click 'Next' again to add the original version and ask the children to read all three. Ask them to TTYP to discuss which version they think is the most effective. Make sure they understand you are not looking for a 'right' answer but their own opinions. Choose two or three sets of partners to feed back.
- Remind the children that so far, they have looked at how the writer has expanded the noun *man*; the *subject* in the sentence. Explain that there is another noun or noun phrase in the same sentence and this one refers to the *object*.
- Click 'Next' to show more of the sentence from the Anthology and read it aloud to the children. Click 'TOL' to show a TOL bubble and use it to discuss the phrase.
- Say that the writer could have expanded this noun phrase too. Click 'Next' to show an example. Read it aloud to the children. Click 'TOL' and use the TOL bubbles to explain the parts of the sentence that expand the noun phrase. Say that as writers we can create different rhythms, different impact and different images in our readers' minds, just by moving words and phrases around in a sentence.
- Click 'Next' to show a few variations of the sentence with the adjectives and noun phrases re-positioned. Ask the children to read each one out chorally and then to TTYP to discuss which one they find most effective, and why. Collect feedback, making sure that they can give reasons for their opinions.
- Remind the children that as writers, we also have to be careful not to add too many adjectives or too much extra information. Say that short and simple writing can be more effective than sentences overloaded with adjectives and information that may not be necessary.
- Click 'Next' to show an example of an overwritten sentence. Read it out to the children and then ask them to TTYP to discuss how the sentence could be improved by removing some of the adjectives or information. Choose two or three to share their ideas. Type a couple of their suggestions into the editable text box.
- Now ask them to look at the *Grammar: expanded noun phrases* activity on p.5 of their Pupils' Book. Explain the activity and ask them to complete it with their partners. Choose two or three to share their answers. Clarify where necessary.

Homework Book p.4 provides further practice on expanded noun phrases.

What if not...? **PB**

Purpose: for children to consider how character, setting and plot each affects the other

Curriculum link:
drawing inferences and justifying with evidence, identifying key details that support ideas

- Ask the children to look at the What if not...? questions in the Pupils' Book p.6. Model how you consider the first What if not...?: What if not *away*? What if good King Richard *had returned to England*? TOL using your own ideas and/or print the script from the **CD (file 4.2)**.
- Now ask the children to TTYP and discuss this and the other What if not...? questions in the Pupils' Book p.6. Collect feedback and encourage others to build upon the argument. Give your opinion, too.

What do I want? How do I get it? **CD** **A**

Purpose: for children to be able to hypothesise about characters' actions and support their ideas with evidence from the text

- Tell the children that different characters want different things in the story and that some are obvious and some are less obvious. Explain that they are going to explore what different characters want and what they do to get it.

- Display **CD (file 4.3)** to show the *What do I want? How do I get it?* grid.
- TOL as you go through the first two characters (Prince John and Guy of Gisborne), drawing children into your thinking and showing how you find evidence in the Anthology text to support your answers.
- Now ask the children to TTYP to discuss the next two characters and to use their Anthology text to help them. Collect feedback and type responses in the cells.

Daily log

Purpose: for children to keep a personal reading, writing and thinking log in order to record thoughts and ideas for their own writing

- Ask the children to record at least one more What if not...? in their Daily log with some notes about how it would affect characters, plot or setting.

Curriculum link: effective discussion; provide justifications for their views

Big Question ⓒⁿ

Purpose: for children to think about and discuss a philosophical question relating to the work of the day

- Display today's Big Question on the CD (file 4.4):

  Does getting what you want always make you happier?

- Follow the process as explained at the end of Day 1 (p.24).

DAY 5

discuss and evaluate how authors use language

Showing and telling ⓒⁿ

Purpose: for children to be able to identify and evaluate the writer's use of language to create imaginary worlds

- Remind the children that sometimes story writers have to *tell* us things about the places or people they are writing about, but that good writers can also *show* us by using language in interesting ways.
- Display the **CD (file 5.1)** to show the first example of the writer *telling* and *showing*. Use the think bubble to guide you, but add your own comments and draw the children into your TOL.
- Now ask the children to TTYP to decide whether the other extracts are *telling* or *showing*.
- Tell the children to TTYP to decide which of the *showing* pieces of text is the most effective and why. Collect feedback and use it to stimulate discussion.
- Remind the children they should try to use *showing* instead of *telling* sentences in their writing.

making comparisons

Dramatic reconstruction ⓒⁿ

Purpose: for children to develop their understanding of parody

- Tell the children that there are many, many different versions of this legend, including plays, poems, songs, films and TV series.
- Now tell the children that they are going to look at a version which gives a very different account of events. It is called a *parody* or a *spoof* and it is a playscript. Explain that characters in parodies do not behave as we expect them to!
- Display **CD (file 5.2)**, the extract from the parody, and read it out loud to the children.
- Ask them to find the part of the story it is based on (p.5 in the Anthology) and TTYP to discuss how the parody has changed characters and their actions. Collect feedback.

- Now organise the class into fours – two sets of partners. Ask them to find the parody script in the Dramatic reconstruction activity in the Pupils' Book p.6 and to read a part each.
- Tell them they are going to choose another part of the story and work together to plan a short role-play as a Robin Hood parody, following the prompts in the Pupils' Book p.6 as a guide.
- Once they have had time to plan, ask them to perform their role-plays. Walk around listening in, noting good examples of parody and praising good group work.
- Give feedback.

<table>
<tr><td>Curriculum link:
noting ideas</td></tr>
</table>

Daily log

Purpose: for children to keep a personal reading, writing and thinking log in order to record thoughts and ideas for their own writing

- Explain the difference between having *empathy with* and *sympathy for* a character to the children (*Empathy with* – we can understand what a character is feeling and thinking; *sympathy for* – we feel sad/sorry for a character and like/approve of them). Then ask them to record in their Daily log which character they felt most empathy with, or sympathy for, and why.

<table>
<tr><td>effective
discussion; provide
justifications for
their views</td></tr>
</table>

Big Question

Purpose: for children to think about and discuss a philosophical question relating to the work of the day

- Display today's Big Question on the **CD (file 5.3)**:

  Is it important for people to behave as we expect them to?

- Follow the process as explained at the end of Day I (p.24).

 WRITING FICTION

 DAY 6

Build a setting

Purpose: for children to be able to build a setting around one phrase, using figurative language.

<table>
<tr><td>understand,
through being
shown, the skills
and processes
essential for
writing: that is,
thinking aloud to
generate ideas,
drafting, and
re-reading to
check that the
meaning is clear</td></tr>
</table>

- Use the **CD (file 6.1)** to show the part of the story where the phrase 'the trees groaned and the leaves sighed' is used.
- Read it out to the children. Explain that you really like the phrase and the way it makes the trees sound like humans, sympathising with the people of England.
- Say the phrase again, and mimic the sound of a *groan* and a *sigh* as you say those words. Explain that *groaned* and *sighed* are onomatopoeic. Use MT/YT to say the words groaned and sighed encouraging the children to feel and hear how they can be onomatopoeic.
- Explain that you are going to use the phrase to build up the description of a setting. Tell the children that you want create a different atmosphere to the one in the story.
- Display **CD (file 6.2)** and TOL to show the process of building up a setting based on the phrase. Use the think bubbles, but add your own thoughts and ideas as well.
- Now ask the children, either individually or in partners, to compose one or two sentences to describe a sinister forest using the prompts in the Build a setting activity in the Pupils' Book p.7. Do not let the children write until they can say their first sentence out loud.
- Ask partners to take turns to develop each other's sentences. Encourage crossings out, switching words round, etc. Emphasise that this is writing in action – it is not a neat, finished piece of writing!

Contexts

Curriculum link:
discuss and evaluate
how authors use
language

Purpose: for children to develop their understanding of how words can create different effects in different contexts.

• Tell the children that you want to use some of the words from the Build a setting activity to create a completely different setting.

• Explain that you are going to experiment with the words, using them in different sentences.

• Display **CD (file 6.3)** to show the words you want to use and the example sentences. Read them out loud.

• Now ask the children to TTYP to discuss which sentence was the one that created the most effective pictures in their heads. Collect feedback and encourage children to give possible reasons for their choices.

• Tell the children to write two or three sentences that include the same words using the instructions in the Contexts activity in the Pupils' Book p.7 and their partners to help them.

Daily log

ask questions to
improve their
understanding,
provide
justifications for
their views

Purpose: for children to keep a personal reading, writing and thinking log in order to record thoughts and ideas for their own writing

• Ask the children to think about which character in the Robin Hood legend they would most like to meet. Tell them to write in their Daily log at least two questions they would like to ask them and then write the answers they think the character might give.

Big Question

effective
discussion; provide
justifications for
their views

Purpose: for children to develop their skills of argument and discussion through a mini enquiry session based on a philosophical question relating to the work of the day

• Display today's Big Question on the **CD (6.4)**:

  Do we all need a hero or heroine to look up to?

• Follow the process as explained at the end of Day I(p.24).

DAY 7

Grammar: colons, dashes and semicolons

**Year 6
Grammar**
use of the
semicolon, colon
and dash to
indicate a stronger
subdivision

Purpose: for children to revise their existing knowledge of punctuation and its purpose. To develop their awareness of punctuation to indicate stronger subdivisions than commas

Colons

• Tell the children that when we speak we use our voices to convey meaning, using different tones, silences and pauses. We also use facial expressions and body language. Say that when we write, we have to use the little marks we call punctuation to show readers when to stop, start, pause, wait in suspense and recognise that someone is speaking.

• Tell them that you are going to give a little speech and you want them to picture where they would add full stops, commas, exclamation marks, question marks or inverted commas, if the speech were written down.

• Read the speech below quite slowly, with appropriate fluency and expression to indicate where punctuation marks would be necessary if it were written down:

  You are an amazing group of children, eager to work and learn!
  "What are we doing today?" you ask.
  Well (if all goes to plan) this is what we are going to do today...

Context

Purpose: for children to learn about the historical context of the story

- Tell the children that like myths and fairy tales, legends reflect how people looked and behaved in particular places and times.
- Explain that no one knows exactly when or where Robin Hood lived or even whether he was a real person, but that stories about the man of the forest dressed in green have been told and listened to for about seven hundred years.
- Now display **CD (file 2.3)** to show the comic strip and captions about the time and setting of the legend of Robin Hood.
- Read the text out loud with appropriate emphasis and intonation.

Read a story version 3

> *explain and discuss their understanding of what they have read*

Purpose: for children to hear and enjoy the full version of the story for the first time

- Tell the children they are now going to hear the whole story for the very first time. Show your enthusiasm before you start. TOL about which parts you can't wait to hear about, etc.
- Read the complete text from the Anthology (p. 4) to the children with great enjoyment. Use appropriate intonation and body language to add to your storytelling 'performance'!
- At the end of the story, ask the children to TTYP to discuss the Read a story version 3 activity questions in the Pupils' Book p.4. Then collect feedback.

Daily log

> *summarising the main ideas*

Purpose: for children to keep a personal reading, writing and thinking log in order to record thoughts and ideas for their own writing

- Tell the children to create a mind map of the characters and the settings in the story. They should have a 'branch' for each character and for each setting.

Big Question

> *effective discussion; provide justifications for their views*

Purpose: for children to develop their skills of argument and discussion through a mini enquiry session based on a philosophical question relating to the work of the day

- Display today's Big Question on the **CD (file 2.4)**:

  Is everyone capable of being a hero?

- Follow the process as explained at the end of Day 1 (p.24).

DAY 3

Word power 2

> *exploring the meaning of words in context*

Purpose: for children to develop their knowledge and application of rarer vocabulary taken from the text; for children to understand how writers use language for effect

> barbaric   emerged   inhospitable   tedious   eliminated   tyrant

- Tell the children that the writer of *Robin Hood* and the *Golden Arrow* has used a mixture of informal, everyday spoken language and words and phrases that are not commonly used in everyday conversations.
- Display the Word power 2 words and their definitions on the **CD (file 3.1)**. Look at the words with the children and then read the sentences to them. Ask the children to repeat the sentences using MT/YT, giving dramatic emphasis and actions as you say them.

Build a story 1

Purpose: for children to be able to see a story grow through three stages of development

- Remind the children that they *heard* two versions of the legend of *Robin Hood and the Golden Arrow* (Story versions 1 & 2) before they *heard* and *read* the full story. It prepared them to *read* the full story.
- Explain that you are going to show them two versions of a new story to be written. These versions prepared the writer to *write* the full story. You are in the role of the writer of this story during these activities.
- Display the **CD (file 7.2)** and explain that these were the questions that helped you to know what to put in the new story.
- Now display **CD (file 7.3)** Build a story 1.
- Read it out loud to the children. Explain that you are now going to show them another version of the new story to be written. This one has additional information and words – it has been developed.

Build a story 2

Purpose: for children to be able to see a story grow through three stages of development

- Display **CD (file 7.4)** Build a story 2 and read it out loud to the children.
- Click 'Highlights' and TOL using the highlighted text showing additional information, synonyms and adjectives as you compare this version with Build a story 1.

Build a story 3

Purpose: for children to see an example of writing that will provide a model for their own writing

- An example story is provided as a model for writing. You are still in the role of writer.
- Display **CD (file 7.5)** to show Build a story 3. Explain that when writing this story, you were in the role of Lady Marian. Read 'your' story (Build a story 3) to the children.
- Print out a copy of the story from the **CD (file 7.6)** for each set of partners. Ask the children to evaluate your writing using the questions. Encourage them to highlight/underline and annotate the text. Collect feedback. Then ask the children to highlight any punctuation marks for a colon, semicolon or dash in the text. Tell them to TTYP to discuss what effect they have on the way they read the text. Choose two or three to feed back.

Daily log

Purpose: for children to keep a personal reading, writing and thinking log in order to record thoughts and ideas for their own writing

- Ask the children to take turns to read a section each of Build a story 3 and then share ideas for a title for the story. Ask them to record their best idea in their Daily log and explain why they think it is a good title.

Big Question

Purpose: for children to think about and discuss a philosophical question relating to the work of the day

- Display today's Big Question on the **CD (file 7.7)**:

  Is putting yourself in danger brave or foolish?

- Follow the process as explained at the end of Day 1 (p.24).

Curriculum link:
plan writing by noting and developing ideas; consider how authors have developed characters and settings

understand, through being shown, the skills and processes essential for writing

noting ideas, provide justifications for their views

effective discussion; provide justifications for their views

DAY 8

Curriculum link:
plan writing
by noting and
developing
ideas; consider
how authors
have developed
characters

Write a story 1

Purpose: to develop children's confidence and skills in story planning and development

- Tell the children they are going to be writing in the role of Sir Guy of Gisborne. Remind them that cruel Prince John gave Sir Guy and his friend the Sheriff of Nottingham power to collect money and land from the poor people of Nottingham. Ask them to find the following sections in the Anthology and follow the text as you read it out loud, to remind themselves of his part in the story.

  'They taxed and fined and robbed their Saxon subjects' to '…was cheated of his father's land by Gisborne' *on p.4 and from:*

  "I've a score to settle with you, you thief!" *to* 'This time his blade shaved the hair from Robin's neck' *on p.12.*

- Tell them that Partner 1 is now Sir Guy and Partner 2 is now the Sheriff of Nottingham and they are going to have a discussion about the mysterious man in green who robs the rich to give to the poor.
- Display **CD (file 8.1)** to show these guide questions to stimulate a short role-play. Walk around and listen in:
  - Why do you both dislike Robin Hood so much?
  - Why do you think he is so keen to help the poor?
  - What could you do to trick him into coming to the castle in Nottingham?
- Give feedback on good discussions.
- Now show **CD (file 8.2)** Write a story 1 – the pre-prepared 'bare bones' version of Gisborne's story.

Write a story 2

Purpose: to develop children's confidence and skills in story planning and development

- TOL as you model on a flipchart, or large sheet of paper, how to develop sentence 1 by adding some more information, adjectives, adverbs and a synonym. The **CD (file 8.3)** gives an example to use if you prefer or if you want to show two examples.
- Repeat with sentence 2 using your own ideas and/or **CD (file 8.4)** if you prefer.
- Now tell the children they are going to develop 3, 4 and 5 using points A to D in the Write a story 2 activity in the Pupils' Book p.9. Remind them that they can keep changing their sentences until they are happy with them. It is writing in action, not a finished piece of work.

provide reasoned
justifications for
their views

Daily log

Purpose: for children to keep a personal reading, writing and thinking log in order to record thoughts and ideas for their own writing

- Remind the children that many books, plays, films and TV series have been made about Robin Hood. Ask them to TTYP to discuss why they think this legend is so popular. Ask them to record at least three reasons in their Daily log.

effective
discussion; provide
justifications for
their views

Big Question

Purpose: for children to think about and discuss a philosophical question relating to the work of the day

- Display today's Big Question on the **CD (file 8.5)**:

  Can we ever know the truth about another person?*

- Follow the process as explained at the end of Day 1 (p.24).

  * This Big Question will be revisited on Day 11 – the first day of the non-fiction week (p.38).

Curriculum link:
describing settings,
characters and
atmosphere
and integrating
dialogue

Write a story 3 🅿🅱

*Purpose: for children to use the sentences they have already developed to write their full, first
person narrative version of Sir Guy's story*

- Tell the children that they are ready to write their own story from Sir Guy's point
  of view. Ask them to use the sentences they have already developed and the
  guidance in the Write a story 3 activity in the Pupils' Book p.9.
- Remind them to:
  - remember the work that they did in Build a setting on Day 6
  - use any useful parts of their Daily log to help them
  - look at the word wall for Power words and phrases
  - use a thesaurus to find synonyms
  - use *showing* rather than *telling* sentences.

- Encourage children to rehearse their opening sentence with their partners before
  they begin to write.

assessing the
effectiveness of
their own and
others' writing

Share a story

Purpose: for children to read and share their full stories

- Ask the children to read through their own story, underlining their favourite or
  best parts. Ask them to share these with their partners. Collect feedback on the
  best bits from partners.
- Make sure that any powerful or rarer words or phrases are written on cards and
  added to the word wall.

Evaluate and edit 🅒🅓

*Purpose: for children to evaluate their own and their partner's work against specific criteria
and then discuss how they could improve their work*

- Display **CD (file 10.1)** to show the evaluation prompts and read them together
  using MT/YT.
- As a model, select an example of work from the children where the writing has met
  the criteria, and share this with the other children, explaining why it works well.
- Tell the children to take turns to read their partner's writing and discuss how well
  they have met the criteria.
- Ask children to discuss at least two changes they could make to improve their
  work following the partner discussion.

proofread for
spelling and
punctuation errors

Proofread

*Purpose: for children to proofread their work and make changes to improve the accuracy of
their grammar, punctuation and spelling*

- Now ask the children to proofread their work. If you have noticed that several
  children need to improve on a particular aspect of spelling, grammar or
  punctuation, use this as a focus for the Proofread activity. Write an example which
  includes common errors from the children's writing and use this as a model.
- The children should always be checking for standard use of punctuation and
  correct spelling of common exception words.
- The following points would be relevant as the particular focus for this Unit:
  - check that the first person and past tense have been used consistently
  - check the spelling of more ambitious vocabulary choices
  - check correct use of punctuation for effect, e.g. exclamation marks.

Very Big Question

Purpose: for the children to develop or revise their opinions through the exploration of one of the Big Questions in more depth

- Explain to the children that they are going to vote to choose one of the Big Questions they have discussed to explore further in this lesson.
- Tell the children the "rules" for the Very Big Question time:

  Think before you talk. Wait for others to finish before you talk. Good listening.

- Display the Big Question they have voted for on the **CD** (select from the Big Question files for Unit 1). Give everyone some time to think about the question. Ask partners to share their thoughts on the question.
- Allow each child to express their opinion. Encourage responses from children to what has been said rather than insisting that each child speaks in turn. Step in to clarify, paraphrase or draw in children who are reluctant to talk.
- As the 'enquiry' develops and changes direction, pause the proceedings occasionally and re-frame the question – remember the Big Question is a starting point for genuine enquiry. Repeat thinking time and TTYP to refresh the process and to prevent one or two children dominating.
- Allow time to have a final round where children are asked to think about what has been said and share how their opinion has changed or not as a result of the discussion.

Journalistic writing

READING AND WRITING NON-FICTION

The non-fiction part of the Unit introduces children to different types of journalistic texts to examine bias and balance, formal and informal writing. The children will examine the audience and purpose of the writing. The activities build up to the children writing and presenting their own TV news report covering the drama of Maid Marian's wedding.

See p.20 for the daily timetable for the Non-fiction week.

Non-fiction

Reading

Children will:

- read a range of journalistic writing and determine its purpose and audience
- understand the importance of the five Ws – *Who? What? When? Where?* and *Why?* in journalistic writing and identify them in a range of articles
- identify when journalistic writing is neutral or biased.

Writing

Key writing purpose to be shared with the children:

To write a TV broadcast reporting on Maid Marian's wedding and deliver it to the class.

Writing evaluation to be shared with the children

My broadcast:

- has a neutral tone, avoiding showing bias
- answers the five Ws (*Who? What? When? Where? Why?*)
- when presented, engages my audience because I use varied intonation and facial expressions.

Grammar:

- uses the past tense for the report.

See the Planning section of the Software ('Timetables' tab) for a printable version of the Writing purpose and evaluation.

Non-fiction: Journalistic writing

Introduction

Purpose: for children to revise their knowledge of journalistic texts

- Show the Big Question from Day 8, *Can we ever know the truth about another person?* on the **CD (file 8.5)**.
- Ask the children to TTYP to recall some of the points they discussed and ideas they explored. Collect feedback.
- Remind the children that the narrator in Geraldine McCaughrean's version of *Robin Hood and the Golden Arrow* shows us a particular point of view about the characters and events. Is this the truth about Robin Hood?
- Display the final section on the **CD (file 11.1)** or print a copy of this from the **CD (file 11.2)** and read aloud to the children giving emphasis to the words that are in bold.
- Ask the children to TTYP to say what the narrator thinks about Robin Hood and Prince John and his men.
- Collect feedback. Expand on their ideas, clarifying that the narrator of the legend of *Robin Hood and the Golden Arrow is biased*. The narrator presents Robin Hood as a hero who has faults but whose heart was in the right place, while Prince John, the Sheriff of Nottingham and Sir Guy of Gisborne are shown as totally cruel and hard-hearted villains.
- Explain that in journalistic writing, some reports, articles or interviews are *biased* and some are *objective* or *neutral*.
- Tell the children that if a journalist was writing about Robin Hood robbing the rich to feed the poor, they might choose to give a more *balanced* point of view about events or the report might be biased in favour of Prince John and his men!
- Explain that there are many forms of journalistic writing, such as news reports, interviews, articles and reviews.
- Explain that journalistic writing can be experienced in:
  - print form, e.g. newspapers and magazines
  - on screen, e.g. TV, teletext and the Internet
  - in audio form, e.g. the radio.
- Hold up the five Ws – Who? What? Where? When? and Why? printed from **CD (file 11.3)** and remind the children that these questions are the basis for journalistic writing.
- Display the five Ws on your 'journalistic' writing word wall.

Word power

Purpose: for children to become familiar with some words and synonyms associated with journalistic texts

> *media   broadcast   biased   neutral*

- Display the words and their definitions from the **CD (file 11.4)**. Explain that they are words that will help us to identify, talk about and write journalistic texts. Read each word and sentence to the children. Ask the children to repeat the sentences using MT/YT.
- Print out the words and definitions from the **CD (file 11.5)** and display the words and definitions on your 'journalistic' word wall. Find opportunities to use the words yourself during the day, e.g. 'I don't want to broadcast my mistake to the whole school! I always try to be *neutral* when I mark your work!' and encourage the children to use them in their everyday conversation.
- Now tell the children to do the Word power activity in the Pupils' Book p.10.

Journalistic texts

Purpose: for children to be able to recognise a variety of print media texts

Curriculum link: read a range of non-fiction

- Explain that one method of mass communication is through *print media* i.e. reports, articles, interviews and reviews printed on paper in the form of magazines and newspapers.
- Ask the children to look at the examples of journalistic writing in the Journalistic texts activity in the Pupils' Book p.10. Read them out loud.
- Now ask the children to match up the examples A, B and C with the print media types 1, 2 and 3. Collect feedback and clarify where necessary.

Five Ws

Purpose: for children to be able to identify the five Ws of journalism

learn the conventions of different types of writing, identifying key details

- Point to the five Ws on your word wall and remind the children that journalists use these to organise information in their reports and articles.
- Give each child a copy of the five Ws grid from printable **CD (file 11.6)**. Explain that they are going to use the grid to identify the five Ws in text C – the news report about the cat and the washing (Journalistics texts, Pupils' Book p.11).
- Tell the children to TTYP to re-read text C. Display the grid on the **CD (file 11.7)**. Click 'Complete' to reveal the answer for the first of the Ws.
- Now tell them to discuss which parts of the text show the other four Ws. Explain that sometimes there will be more than one example for each W!
- Ask the children to fill in their grids once they agree.
- When they have completed their grids, display text C on the **CD (file 11.8)** and collect feedback. Identify key parts of the text and TOL to correct any misconceptions.

Daily log

Purpose: for children to keep a personal reading, writing and thinking log in order to record thoughts and ideas for their own writing

provide reasoned justifications for their views

- Tell the children to TTYP to discuss why hearing, watching or reading the news is important. Tell them to record at least three reasons why we should keep up to date with the news.

DAY 12

Deconstruction 1

Purpose: for children to be able to identify the main points of a more complex news report and to be able to identify bias

identifying key details; evaluate how authors use language, considering the impact on the reader

- Ask the children to look at the *Sherwood Bugle* text 'Hood Gang Behind Gold Theft?' in the Anthology p.14. Tell them to follow the text as you read it out loud with lots of expression.
- Do a quick vocabulary check for these words, explaining their meaning in the context of this text:
  - *scouring* – searching every corner, nook and cranny
  - *intercepted* – caught, ambushed
  - *notorious* – villainous, well-known for being bad.
- Explain that the style and language in this report is more complex than the 'Cat's Crime…' text and it is harder to identify the five Ws.
- Ask Partner 1 to read the first section of the text and Partner 2 to summarise orally the basic information in the report. Remind them to use any of the five Ws to structure their summary. Swap roles for each section.
- Ask them to fill in the five Ws grid from printable **CD (file 12.1)**. Collect feedback.

- Point to the word *neutral* and its definition on your word wall. Remind the children that news should be presented in a balanced, neutral report, but that this doesn't always happen.
- Ask the children to TTYP to decide whether the *Sherwood Bugle* report is *neutral* or *biased* – point to the word *biased* and its definition on your word wall as you say it.
- Collect feedback and ask for examples from the text to 'prove' it is a biased report, e.g. the emotive words and phrases such as:

'...our great Prince John has worked so hard...' 'Brave soldiers...' '...cowardly, armed criminals...' and the mismatch between the title's question and the statement:

'There can be little doubt that the raid was the work of the notorious Robin Hood gang...'

Curriculum link:
understand, through being shown, the skills and processes essential for writing

Write a news report 1 (CD) 🛆

Purpose: for children to develop their ability to write an unbiased news report for a particular audience.

- Tell the children that the editor of the newspaper has asked for a re-write of the report to appear on the children's section of the newspaper's website. She wants a more neutral account of the events and she wants the style and language to be more appropriate for young readers.
- Display the sample sentence on the **CD (file 12.2)**. Use TOL as you model how to change the syntax and vocabulary to suit the audience and to give a more balanced account of events.
- Ask the children to re-read this sentence from the text in the Anthology p.14:

'The heavily protected convoy, on its way to deliver gold and jewels to the castle of our much loved local leader, His Excellency the Sheriff of Nottingham, was intercepted at 6.35p.m. by a group of cowardly, armed criminals, who overpowered the guards before making off with the entire cargo.'

- Now ask them to TTYP to discuss ways of changing this sentence to make it simpler and more neutral.
- Collect feedback and scribe their ideas on to the **CD (file 12.3)** into the blank boxes, and draw arrows to point to the appropriate places in the text where the changes would be made. Correct any misunderstandings about bias and neutrality where necessary and keep reminding the children about their target readers.
- Ask the children to write a simpler and less biased version of the final section of the text, below the sub-heading *Terror*. Remind them to use the 5 Ws (What, Who, Where, When, Why) to help them and to TTYP to share ideas before writing anything down.

noting and developing initial ideas

Daily log

Purpose: for children to keep a personal reading, writing and thinking log in order to record thoughts and ideas for their own writing

- Tell the children to start to design a children's webpage for the newspaper the *Sherwood Bugle*. They could look at the children's BBC *Newsround* website (http://news.bbc.co.uk/cbbcnews) to give them some ideas. This activity will be continued on Day 13.

DAY 13

Curriculum link:
identifying how
language, structure
and presentation
contribute to
meaning

Deconstruction 2

Purpose: for children to be able to be able to recognise stylistic features of informal magazine articles

- Ask the children to TTYP to think about which celebrities regularly appear in newspapers and magazines. Ask them to say what they think they are famous for.
- Tell the children that as well as reports about events that have happened, newspapers and, more often, magazines, have articles based on something that might happen. These are often based on rumours about the lives of celebrities.
- Explain that in order to entertain and interest readers, some magazine journalists use a chatty, *informal* style of writing that is very different to the *formal* style of most news reports.
- Ask the children to follow the text of the magazine article from *Good Day!* magazine in the Anthology p.15 as you read it out loud with appropriate intonation and enthusiasm.
- Display the **CD (file 13.1)** to show the list of stylistic features. Check that the children understand the terminology, e.g. *colloquialisms*. Ask them to TTYP to discuss what they think is the opinion expressed in the first paragraph and how is it disguised as fact. Collect feedback and make sure they have noted ambiguous phrases such as *could soon be* and *sources suggest*.
- Repeat the process for the other four stylistic features listed. Encourage lots of TTYP and discussion about the intended *effect* of the features rather than simply finding examples.
- Now ask the children to read alternate sections of the article with their partners.
- Ask them to TTYP to discuss what they think the purpose of the article is, e.g. to entertain, inform, persuade readers to buy the next issue – refer them to the third paragraph. ('Meanwhile if you want to be as fit...')

summarising
the main ideas,
developing ideas

Write a news report 2

Purpose: for children to be able to use the stylistic features and language of an informal magazine article as a model for their own writing

- Play the video on **CD (file 13.2)** of a TV interview with a 21st century Robin Hood denying rumours of a wedding.
- Tell the children that they are journalists for *Hi There!* magazine – a rival to *Good Day!* and they are going to write an article based on the information in Robin's TV interview.
- Explain that you are going to replay the interview and they are going to make some notes on what they think are the main points.
- Now ask them to TTYP to read the transcript of the TV interview in the Anthology p.16, reading a section each in turn and then working with their partners to check their notes against the transcript, adding to or changing their notes where necessary.
- Collect feedback and display the **CD (file 13.3)**. TOL and click 'Complete' to model turning notes into an article in a similar style to the *Good Day!* text.
- Now tell them to re-read the *Good Day!* article in the Anthology p.15 as a reminder of the style of writing that is appropriate for their article. Ask them to look at the completed examples on the **CD (file 13.3)** to help them to write their article for rival *Hi There!* magazine.

Non-fiction: Journalistic writing

Daily log

Purpose: for children to keep a personal reading, writing and thinking log in order to record thoughts and ideas for their own writing

- Tell the children to continue working on a design for a children's webpage for the newspaper the *Sherwood Bugle* (see Daily log activity Day 12, page 40).

DAY 14

Curriculum link: summarising the main ideas, making comparisions

Deconstruction 3 (CD)

Purpose: for children to be able to identify the commentator and a participant in a news event and be able to comment upon the differences between them

- Tell the children they are now going to hear a 'live' radio broadcast of Lady Marian's wedding.
- Make sure they understand the difference between a live broadcast and commentary in the present tense and a report given after the event in the past tense.
- Play the audio on **CD (file 14.1)**. Encourage the children to try to picture the scene and events in their heads as they listen.
- Ask the children to TTYP to summarise the events they have just heard.
- Now ask them to TTYP to discuss what the role of the commentator is. Collect feedback, making sure they understand that they are *outside* the action, i.e. there to comment on what they see for the audience (who are also outside the action).
- Explain that you are going to play the commentary again and that you now want the children to take notes about the events as they listen.
- Organise the children into fours. Tell them that they are going to plan and act out a short role-play of the wedding and the commentary. The roles will be:

  Lady Marian, Sir Guy, intruder (Robin Hood), radio commentator. Lady Marian will also play the role of a reporter who interviews Sir Guy after the 'kidnap'.

- Give feedback on the groups' performances and ask the children to TTYP to discuss the difference between the commentator's role and the other roles. Collect feedback making sure they understand that the commentators were outside the action and the others were inside the action or events.

retrieve, record and present information from non-fiction

Write a news report 3 (CD)

Purpose: for children to develop their ability to adapt the language and form of a text to suit a different purpose and audience

- Tell the children that they are going to use a transcript of some of the live radio commentary and their role-plays to help them to write a TV news report about the events.
- Ask them to TTYP to remind each other of the difference between a live commentary and a report after an event has happened.
- Display the diagram on the **CD (file 14.2)** and TOL as you model how to:
  - identify and use the 5 Ws
  - change tenses
  - adapt language
  - alter format

  to create a short TV news script. Click 'Reveal' on the first screen to complete the TV news report entries and navigate to the second screen to model the process by typing your own text into the boxes.
- Ask the children to write their own TV news report on the wedding.

Curriculum link:
proofread for
spelling and
punctuation errors

Proofread

Purpose: for children to proofread their work and make changes to improve the accuracy of their grammar, punctuation and spelling

- Now ask the children to proofread their work. If you have noticed that several children need to improve on a particular aspect of spelling, grammar or punctuation, use this as a focus for the Proofread activity. Write an example which includes common errors from the children's writing and use this as a model.
- The children should always be checking for standard use of punctuation and correct spelling of common exception words.
- The following points would be relevant as the particular focus for this Unit:
  - check that the news report is consistently written in the past tense
  - check that quotations are punctuated correctly
  - check for use of capital letters for proper nouns.

Daily log

Purpose: for children to keep a personal reading, writing and thinking log in order to record thoughts and ideas for their own writing

- Ask the children to TTYP to discuss what else they would include in a TV news item, e.g. graphics, background information about the people involved, short interviews with guests, in the studio or by satellite link or outside broadcasts, etc.

TV news presentations

Purpose: for children to have the opportunity to complete and present their TV news presentations to a small group and complete self- and peer-assessments

- Give the children time to complete and refine their TV news reports.
- If they wish they can enlist the help of other children (maximum of two) to hold up graphics or improvise being interviewees if required.
- Organise the children into groups of four or six.
- Explain that they are going to take turns to take the role of a newsreader and perform their news report of the wedding to the rest of the group as if they were presenting to a camera in a TV studio.
- Remind them of the need to not only *inform* their audience but also to engage and interest them using varied intonation and facial expression as they deliver their reports.
- Walk round keeping the groups on track with timing. Note points for positive feedback on quality of news reports, performance, good listening, good organisation of group roles, etc.

perform their own
compositions,
using appropriate
intonation,
volume, and
movement so that
meaning is clear

assessing the
effectiveness of
their own and
others' writing

Evaluate and edit (CD)

Purpose: for children to evaluate their own and their partner's work against specific criteria and then discuss how they could improve their work

- Display **CD (file 15.1)** to show the evaluation prompts and read them together using MT/YT.
- As a model, select an example of a presentation where the children met the criteria, and share with the other children why it worked well.
- Tell the children to discuss with their partner how well they met the criteria.
- Ask children to discuss at least two changes they could make to improve their presentation following the partner discussion.

DAY 15

Poetry: The power of imagery
Non-fiction: Argument

Timetable

WEEK 1 **Reading poetry** **The power of imagery** – 'Rabbit in Mixer Survives'

Day 1	Day 2	Day 3	Day 4	Day 5
The poetry store	Zoom in on poetic terms	Word power 1	Zoom in on character	What if not...?
Introducing the poem 1	Introducing the poem 3	Re-read the poem	Drama storyboard	Word power 2
Think and link 1	Clarify and identify	Read and compare images 🖶	Daily log	Daily log
Introducing the poem 2	Think and link 2	Daily log	Big Question	Big Question
Daily log	Daily log	Big Question		
Big Question	Big Question			

WEEK 2 **Writing poetry** **The power of imagery** – 'Rabbit in Mixer Survives'

Day 6	Day 7	Day 8	Day 9	Day 10
Build an image – personification	Build a poem 1	Write a poem 1 🖶	Write a poem 3	Read and share
Extend the metaphor	Build a poem 2	Write a poem 2		Evaluate and edit
Build a form	Build a poem 3 🖶	Daily log		Proofread
Daily log	Daily log	Big Question		Very Big Question
Big Question	Big Question			

WEEK 3 **Reading and writing non-fiction** Argument

Day 11	Day 12	Day 13	Day 14	Day 15
Linking the texts	Deconstruction 1	Scoring 'Animals rule!' – Deconstruction 2	Deconstruction 3	Present the argument
Word power 🖶	Read an argument 🖶	Planning an argument	Write debate materials 🖶	Evaluate and edit
Audience and purpose	Daily log	Daily log	Proofread	Broadcast
Grammar: layout devices				
Daily log	Daily log	Daily log		

🖶: shows that a file should be printed out from the Software.

Overview of the Unit

This Unit explores the power of imagery using 'Rabbit in Mixer Survives' by Roger McGough as its focus. 'Pike' by Ted Hughes, 'The Sea' by James Reeves and 'Fog' by Carl Sandburg provide ample material for exploring metaphor and simile. By the end of this Unit children will be able to create their own extended metaphors and have a firm grasp of how a poet creates layered images.

In the non-fiction part of the Unit children will examine the audience and purpose of argument texts and how pejorative and emotive language is used. They read a discursive text that explores whether or not animals should rule the planet. The children will practise creating balanced arguments as well as exploring how to organise a persuasive paragraph. For more information about the Non-fiction week and the Non-fiction writing evaluation criteria, see p.59.

The Homework Book provides a homework activity related to the content of this Unit for each of the three weeks.

Fiction

Reading

Children will:

- read a range of poems, and make connections with other poems they have read and their own experiences
- through exploration of 'Rabbit in Mixer Survives' by Roger McGough, understand that ballads or narrative poems tell a story and have a particular form
- understand that imagery is created and enhanced in poetry using specific techniques, e.g *extended metaphor, personification, onomatopoeia* and *simile*
- develop their understanding of the plot of 'Rabbit in Mixer Survives' by retelling the story and selecting the most important events.

Writing

Key writing purpose to be shared with the children:

To write a poem in free verse which describes a sea creature, using extended metaphor and personification.

Writing evaluation to be shared with the children

My poem:

- creates unusual images, to make the reader see my creature differently
- describes the sea creature using simile, extended metaphor and personification
- experiments with rhythm by using repetition, alliteration and onomatopoeia.

See the Planning section of the Software ('Timetables' tab) for a printable version of the Writing purpose and evaluation.

Poetry: The power of imagery
'Rabbit in Mixer Survives' by Roger McGough

READING FICTION

Resources
- PB Pupils' Book, pp.12–22
- A Anthology, pp.18–23
- CD CD on interactive whiteboard (Unit 2)
- GB Grammar Bank on CD
- HB Homework Book, pp.8–10

DAY 1

Curriculum link:
read and discuss an increasingly wide range of poetry

The poetry store

Purpose: for children to develop an awareness of how poets use language to create imagery

- You may wish to set up a poetry area for this Unit. The children's section of the online poetry archive has a good selection of poems which can be searched by poet, form and theme. The main poem in this Unit is by Roger McGough, who has published many books for children and more can be learnt about him on his website.
- Use the mind map on the **CD (file 1.1)** to brainstorm any prior knowledge the children have about poetry. Try to tease out any technical language that they remember such as *stanza, line, rhythm, rhyme, alliteration,* etc. Save your changes.
- Display and read aloud the poems in the Poetry store on the **CD (file 1.2)**. The children may enjoy listening to the poems with their eyes shut so that they can really delve into their imaginations. After listening to each poem ask the children to TTYP (Turn to your partner) and discuss the images they saw during the reading. Take feedback and note any particularly vivid images.
- Tell the children they are now going to hear the bare bones of a poem about a rabbit.

Introducing the poem 1 CD

Purpose: for children to become familiar with the bare bones of the poem

- Read Introducing the poem 1 aloud all the way through to the children. Check that they understand all the language.

Introducing the poem 1

The young rabbits asked Grandad Rabbit to tell them a story – the one he's told before about the struggle and the battle. The old rabbit agreed and drifted back in his mind to earlier times, to a place far from home, where the ground had suddenly collapsed beneath him.

But the young rabbits weren't listening. There were murmurs of "Poor old Grandad!" Then they went away and left him on his own, trapped by his memories.

- Use MT/YT (My turn/Your turn), for each point. This is to help the children 'hold' the basic idea in their heads.
- Now display Introducing the poem 1 on the **CD (file 1.3)**.

making comparisons, discussing themes

Think and link 1 CD

Purpose: for children to make links and connections about the imagery in this poem and the poems in the poetry store

- For this activity you are going to look at the poems from the poetry store. Tell the children that poets use imagery to create images, atmosphere and ideas in poems. Explain that the term imagery is often used to describe the images, atmospheres and emotions evoked by poets using these poetic features. Now say that you are going to zoom in on the imagery of stillness in the poems in the poetry store.
- Display the poetry store on the **CD (file 1.4)** and focus on three key images:
  - 'Fog': the way that the poet describes the fog as 'sitting on silent haunches'.
  - Explain that haunches are the back legs of a four legged animal.

- Display **CD (file 7.1)** to show the speech written down. Ask the children to follow the text on the screen as you read it aloud with the same fluency and expression you used before. Point to each punctuation mark as you read.
- Explain that as writers, we might want to divide a sentence with something stronger than a comma. If so, we can use a special punctuation mark called a *colon*.
- Click 'Next' to show where a colon has been used to replace one of the commas in the text. Say that the colon indicates a more obvious pause here now, but more importantly, it is a sign showing us that more information is to follow.
- Explain that if a colon is used, the part of the sentence before the colon (the clause) *must* make sense on its own. Click 'Next' to show the speech again. Click 'Highlight' to show the main clause in the sentence, highlighted and then isolated. Ask the children to check it makes sense on its own.
- Tell the children that the writer Geraldine McCaughrean has used colons in specific places in the story *Robin Hood and the Golden Arrow*. Click 'Next' to show an extract from the text. Read it out to the children, pointing to the colon in the sentence. Click 'TOL' and use the TOL bubbles to explain why the writer has used a colon instead of a comma.
- Click 'Next' again to show the sentence with the colon replaced by a comma. Click 'TOL' and use the TOL bubble to explain that this impact is reduced in this version.
- Click 'Next' to show the extract again. Ask the children to TTYP to identify the clause before the colon and to check it makes sense. Choose two sets of partners to feed back. Click 'Highlight' to highlight the clause for clarification.
- Now ask them to look at section A of the Grammar: colons, dashes and semicolons activity on p.8 of their Pupils' Book. Explain the activity and ask them to complete it with their partners. Choose two or three to share their answers. Clarify where necessary, making sure they can identify the clause before the colon in each sentence.

Dashes

- Explain that another way we can indicate a pause that is stronger than a comma, but not as final or powerful as a full stop, is a *dash*. Click 'Next' to show another extract.
- Read it out to the children, pointing to the dash in the sentence. Use the TOL bubbles to TOL about why the writer has used a dash instead of a comma.
- Now ask them to look at section B of the Grammar: colons, dashes and semicolons activity on p.8 of their Pupils' Book. Explain the activity and ask them to complete it with their partners. Choose two or three to share their answers. Clarify where necessary.

Semicolons

- Explain that there is another punctuation mark called a *semicolon* and this is used instead of a full stop, to join what could be two separate sentences.
- Click 'Next' to show an example of a semicolon in an extract from the story. Click 'TOL' and use the think bubble to explain the writer's use of a semicolon to divide a sentence. Ask the children to TTYP to check that *both* parts of the sentence (the two clauses) make sense on their own.
- Click 'Next' again to show the extract written as two separate sentences. Click 'TOL' and use the TOL bubble to explain that the writer could have chosen to write two completely separate sentences instead. Ask the children to TTYP to complete section C on p.8 of their Pupils' Book. Collect answers and clarify if necessary.
- Tell them that they could experiment with punctuation in their own writing by checking whether: *a colon or a dash could replace a comma or a semicolon could be used to link two clauses.*

Homework Book pp.5 and 6 provide further practice on colons, dashes and semicolons.

– 'The Sea': the way that the poet describes the quiet sea:

> But on quiet days in May or June,
> When even the grasses on the dune
> Play no more their reedy tune,
> With his head between his paws
> He lies on the sandy shores,
> So quiet, so quiet, he scarcely snores.

– 'Pike': The way the poet describes the pike in summer:

> No, no! I laze
> Through the blazing June days.
> On, on, all summer
> I sunbathe in bliss
> And gaze at the sky
> And pray to become a
> Dragonfly

- Ask the children to TTYP and discuss the words and phrases that create a sense of stillness. Take feedback.
- Now ask them to TTYP and think about the type of stillness each poem is creating. Take feedback.
- Link this to the image of the final part of Introducing the poem 1 – 'trapped by memories'. Can the children make any connections between the ideas of stillness in the other poems and this one? Ask them to TTYP to discuss the type of stillness that describes the rabbit. Is he lonely? What do they think 'trapped by memories' means?

Curriculum link:
identifying how language, structure and presentation contribute to meaning

Introducing the poem 2 ⓒⅅ

Purpose: for children to examine how Introducing the poem 2 provides additional information for the reader and for children to become more familiar with the ideas and images before they hear the full version

- Read Introducing the poem 2 to the children.

Introducing the poem 2

The young rabbits asked Grandad Rabbit to tell them a story – the one he's told before about the struggle and the battle with the humans. The old rabbit said "All right children, settle down," and drifted back in his mind to when he was a bunny, to one springtime when he'd wandered into the woods. Suddenly, without warning, the ground had given way beneath him.

However, his story was falling on deaf ears. There was tittering and murmurs of "Poor old Grandad."

The young rabbits wanted a new story, so they left the old adventurer on his own, trapped by his memories.

- Re-read it, using exaggerated intonation and emphasis where appropriate. Stop after each section to ask the children if there are any words that tell them more about the old rabbit and how the young rabbits respond to him in the poem. Ask the children to TTYP and then encourage them to feed back their thoughts to the class.
- Now display this version on the **CD (file 1.5)**.
- Click 'Highlights' to show how the poem has changed from Introducing the poem 1.
  – Addition of information about time and place: *springtime, the woods*
  – Addition of information about the rabbits: *tittering, old adventurer*
- TOL and use TTYP to share how this extra information changes the pictures in our minds as we hear the poem.

Poetry: The power of imagery

Curriculum link: drawing inferences and justifying these

Daily log

Purpose: for children to be introduced to the process of keeping a personal log of notes, thoughts and ideas, collected from their reading and discussions, to use in their own writing

- See the Daily log notes on Day 1, Unit 1 (p.24). Explain that they are going to continue to collect thoughts and ideas in their Daily log.
- Ask the children to TTYP to discuss how the young rabbits respond to the old rabbit's story. Why do they think the young rabbits act this way?
- Tell them to write at least one more line to describe the old rabbit sitting alone at the end of the poem.

effective discussion; provide justifications for their views

Big Question

Purpose: for children to develop their deeper thinking skills through a mini enquiry session based on a philosophical question relating to the work of the day

- Display today's Big Question on the **CD (file 1.6)**:

  Does alone mean lonely?

- Ask the children to TTYP to discuss the question. Collect feedback and scribe some responses using the CD writing tool. Tell the children that each day's Big Question and their thoughts on paper will be put in a safe place until the end of week 2. They will then vote on which question to discuss more deeply. See introduction for further notes (p.13).

DAY 2

Zoom in on poetic terms (CD) (PB)

Purpose: for children to revise some poetic features* and become familiar with new poetic language

pupils should be taught the technical and other terms needed for discussing what they hear and read

> *alliteration   repetition   personification   rhythm   rhyme   onomatopoeia   simile   metaphor   imagery*

* *revision of repetition, alliteration, rhyme, rhythm, simile, personification and metaphor.*

- Explain to the children that you are going to explore and explain some special poetic language with them and that using this language will help them to describe the poem more accurately, including their feelings about it and the effects made by the poet. It will also help them think clearly about which poetic effect they want to use when they write their poem later.
- Display the lines from 'The Sea' on the **CD (file 2.1)**. Read the lines of the poem out loud with obvious enjoyment, adding expression and intonation to show further meaning.
- Ask the children to TTYP and discuss any of the poetic features they recognise. The words in bold should help them.
- Now click 'Reveal' to show which of the poetic features appears in each line: *metaphor, rhyme, onomatopoeia, repetition, personification, rhythm, alliteration and imagery*. Check with the children which of the terms they are familiar with and which of them are unsure of. All of them except onomatopoeia and imagery should have been covered in previous years.
- Next click 'TOL' and go through each line using TOL to explain how this feature works in the poem. Do not click the 'TOL' for imagery at this stage.
- Ask the children to look in the Pupils' Book pp.12–13 at the glossary of poetic terms. Display the whole poem 'The Sea' by James Reeves on the **CD (file 1.2** screen 2**)** and ask the children to TTYP and discuss it using the special poetic language. Choose some partners to feed back.

- Now on the **CD (file 2.1)** click 'TOL' to explain how imagery works in the poem. (Note that the eye picture in screen 4 represents the imagery in the poem). Ask the children to TTYP and discuss how they feel about the imagery used to describe the sea. Take feedback. You may wish to refer back to the mind map on the **CD (file 1.1)** and review the poetic terms the children have explored.

Introducing the poem 3

Curriculum link: read and discuss an increasingly wide range of poetry

Purpose: for children to hear and enjoy the full version of the poem for the first time

- Tell the children they are now going to hear the whole poem called 'Rabbit in Mixer Survives' by Roger McGough for the first time. Explain that the poem is inspired by a true story the poet read in a newspaper about a rabbit who survived going through a cement mixing machine. The newspaper report describes how the rabbit was scooped up by a digger with lots of sand and mixed up with water in the cement mixing machine. Then he got encased in a block of cement 18 inches long, managed to claw himself out and was held up to dry in front of the fire, before finally making his escape. In the poem the old rabbit tells his grandchildren about this adventure. TOL about which parts you can't wait to hear about, etc.
- Read aloud the full poem from the Anthology p.18 to the children with great enjoyment and appropriate intonation to really engage them.
- At the end of the poem, ask the children to TTYP to discuss Introducing the poem 3 questions in the Pupils' Book p.14. Then collect feedback.

Clarify and identify

Purpose: to identify and clarify some of the imagery in the poem, linking the words with images and ideas that the reader might have

checking that the poem makes sense to them

- Tell the children that this poem is a ballad or narrative poem because it tells a story, but that it is also full of imagery, which you are going to explore now.
- Display the extracts from the text on the **CD (file 2.2)**.
- Explain the extracts from the poem using TOL to identify some obvious examples of imagery. You can click on 'TOL' to display examples if you wish.
- Now ask the children to choose another piece of imagery from the poem in the Anthology p.18 and TTYP to discuss what the poet has written and what images, ideas or feelings are created.

Think and link 2

summarising the main ideas

Purpose: for children to understand the chronology and main points of the poem

- Display the Poetry map on the **CD (file 2.3)** and go through it using TOL to discuss what the main events are. Draw the children's attention to the three different areas explored in the poem: *1) Grandad Rabbit telling the story, 2) the event of the past, 3) the young rabbits' motivation for getting Grandad to tell the story.*

Daily log

Purpose: for children to keep a personal reading, writing and thinking log in order to record thoughts and ideas for their own writing

- Tell the children to create their own Poetry map for 'Rabbit in Mixer Survives' in their Daily log.

49

Poetry: The power of imagery

Curriculum link:
effective discussion;
provide justifications
for their views

Big Question 🔘

Purpose: for children to develop their deeper thinking skills through a mini enquiry session based on a philosophical question relating to the work of the day

- Display today's Big Question on the **CD (file 2.4)**:

  Which is more important: to have imagination or to be realistic?

- Follow the process as explained at the end of Day 1 (p.48).

DAY 3

exploring the
meaning of words
in context

Word power 1 🔘

Purpose: to understand the difference between metaphor and simile

When spring was king of the seasons	the fog comes on little cat feet
Sharp as the colour of a carrot	Her smile was like a lie
The sea is like a hungry dog	When spring was like a promise
The sea is a hungry dog	

- Remind the children about similes and metaphors. Explain that there are tiny clues to help tell one from the other.
  If one thing is *like* another thing it is a *simile*. Similes usually compare things using 'like' 'as' or 'than'.
  If the poet says something is another thing it is a *metaphor*.
- Show the similes and metaphors on the **CD (file 3.1)**. Read each one and ask the children to TTYP to discuss whether it is a metaphor or a simile.
- Drag each phrase into the correct place, explaining why you are putting it there as you do so. TOL to describe what images each phrase provokes for you.

Re-read the poem

Purpose: for children to gain a deeper understanding of the poem

- Let the children follow their own copy of the poem in the Anthology p.18 as you re-read the full version of the poem aloud with great enthusiasm.
- Now ask the children to read their copy of the poem with their partners, alternate stanzas each, and with great expression! Explain that you will be listening in.

pupils should
be taught the
technical and
other terms
needed for
discussing what
they hear and read

Read and compare images 🔘

Purpose: for children to identify the key poetic features in a variety of poems

- Read the poem 'Fog' by Carl Sandburg and then use the grid on the **CD (file 3.2)** to explore its key features. Click 'Complete' to show examples for each heading.
- Now ask the children to work with their partners and takes turns to read one stanza at a time of 'The Sea' on the **CD (file 3.3)** by James Reeves. Print one grid from the **CD (file 3.4)** for each set of partners.
- Model finding out if it is a metaphor or a simile (you could refer to the Zoom in on poetic terms activity in the Pupils' Book, pp.12–13) and annotate your answer on the grid. Then ask the children to TTYP and find examples for the other headings. Take feedback and annotate the grid.
- Finally, ask the children to complete their grid for 'Rabbit in Mixer Survives'. Take feedback from the children and draw together the activity by focusing on the different ways that the poets use personification in their poems.

Curriculum link:
noting ideas,
provide reasoned
justifications for
their views

Daily log 🅰

Purpose: for children to keep a personal reading, writing and thinking log in order to record thoughts and ideas for their own writing

- Ask the children to look at 'Rabbit in Mixer Survives' in the Anthology p.18 and decide on their favourite words or phrases from the poem and to think about why they like them. Ask them to TTYP to share and then record their answers in their Daily log.

effective
discussion; provide
justifications for
their views

Big Question 🆔

Purpose: for children to develop their deeper thinking skills through a mini enquiry session based on a philosophical question relating to the work of the day

- Display today's Big Question on the **CD (file 3.5)**:

  Should we always be trying to change what we have or accept things the way they are?

- Follow the process as explained at the end of Day 1 (p.48)

DAY 4

drawing inferences
and justifying these
with evidence
from the text

Zoom in on character 🅿🅱

Purpose: for children to use clues in the poem to create a rounded description of the main character

- Ask the children to TTYP and identify the main characters in the poem 'Rabbit in Mixer Survives'. Take feedback.
- Explain that the poem explores the relationship between the rabbits themselves, i.e. the young bunnies and Grandad, as well as the relationship between rabbits and man. Say that they are going to be poetry detectives and explore every clue about Grandad in the poem so that they are able to describe him really well.
- Ask the children to look at the Zoom in on character prompts in the Pupils' Books p.14. Give the children time to read the prompts. Model finding some information about how Grandad Rabbit looks and TOL to say what you infer (explain this means 'work out') from this description. For example: 'When it says he has a wrinkled paw I know he is old, but I can also infer that he might be frail because of his age'.
- Ask the children to work in pairs to find information about Grandad Rabbit. Take feedback and then give the children time to write a short character sketch of the old rabbit in their Daily log.

summarising the
main ideas

Drama storyboard 🅰 🅿🅱

Purpose: for children to understand the plot and key ideas of the poem and explore these further using drama

- Tell the children that they are going to work together to break down the poem into five sections.
- Model finding the first section in the Anthology p.18, which is the first five stanzas. Tell the children that this part of the poem is all about Grandad Rabbit being asked to tell his story by the young bunnies.
- Ask them to read the rest of the poem and then TTYP to discuss where they felt changes in the poem happened. Take feedback making sure that each section has a focus such as: *Grandad Rabbit telling the story/drifting back to the past, the bunnies becoming bored as Grandad Rabbit becomes immersed in the past, the bunnies leaving Grandad Rabbit trapped in his story.* Scribe the main ideas onto the whiteboard or display them so the children can refer to them during the freeze-frame activity.

- Now organise the children into groups of four and ask them to work together to create the five freeze-frames that make up the poem. Ask them to think of an image that they think best sums up each part of the poem. Tell them they need to make that image or scene with their bodies; they can be rabbits, machinery and even the landscape.
- When they have composed the five freeze-frames, ask them to come up with a title for each one that sums it up.
- Now tell the children that they have been asked to turn the poem into a film. They will be the director and it will be their job to make a five frame storyboard to focus on the five most important frames of the film. There is advice to help them in the Pupils' Book p.15.

Curriculum link:
noting ideas

Daily log 🅰

Purpose: for children to deepen their understanding of the poem by increasing familiarity with the text and to record their response to it

- Ask the children to re-read the poem in the Anthology p.18. Tell them to stop to record any thoughts, ideas, questions and favourite bits in their Daily log as they read the text.

effective discussion; provide justifications for their views

Big Question (CD)

Purpose: for children to develop their deeper thinking skills through a mini enquiry session based on a philosophical question relating to the work of the day

- Display today's Big Question on the **CD (file 4.1)**:

  Words or actions, which tell us more?

- Follow the process as explained at the end of Day 1 (p.48).

DAY 5

What if not...? 🅿🅱

Purpose: for children to consider how the characters' actions affect the poem

drawing inferences and justifying with evidence, identifying key details that support ideas

- Ask the children to look at the What if not...? activity in the Pupils' Book p.16. TOL modelling how the story would change if Grandad Rabbit were telling the story for the first time, e.g. he would have the scars to show for his adventure and the young rabbits might react very differently.
- Ask them to record at least one more 'What if not...?' in their Daily log with some notes about how it would affect characters, plot and setting.
- For example: What if not *in the countryside*? What if the warren were *in a city*? What other dangers could the rabbits face? Would the bunnies be more used to humans and danger? How would they react to Grandad Rabbit's tale then?

exploring the meaning of words in context

Word power 2 (CD)

Purpose: for children to explore a character further using metaphor

> *If Grandad Rabbit were a car he'd be a…scuffed up, slightly rusted vintage jeep with worn tyres and dim headlights.*
> *If Grandad Rabbit were a film he'd be…*
> *If Grandad Rabbit were a person he'd be…*
> *If Grandad Rabbit were a drink he'd be…*
> *If Grandad Rabbit were a game he'd be…*
> *If Grandad Rabbit were a piece of clothing he'd be…*

- Tell the children that you are going to explore the metaphors in the poem more closely.
- Explain that Roger McGough creates metaphors in his poem. He says something *is* something else. He calls the digger an 'Iron Monster', the sand 'a quicksand sea', the hole that the rabbit falls into 'Hell', and memories 'carrots'. He calls Grandad Rabbit 'the old campaigner' and 'old adventurer'.
- Tell the children that they are going to play the Metaphor game on the **CD (file 5.1)**, where they create metaphors about Grandad Rabbit.
- Show the first metaphor on the CD: *If Grandad Rabbit were a car he'd be a…scuffed up, slightly rusted vintage jeep with worn tyres and dim headlights.* TOL to explain the metaphor – that the car reflects his age (vintage) and the type of car, a jeep, is used on adventures; it is scuffed and rusted like the rabbit is wrinkled and has dim headlights, just as the rabbit is slightly blind.
- Click 'Prompts' to show the other metaphor game prompts and ask the children to TTYP to come up with a metaphor for each of them. Take feedback, each time asking the children to explain what part of Grandad Rabbit they are reflecting in their imagery.
- N.B. One of the metaphors is personification – personification is a type of metaphor – keep an eye out to see if any of the pupils notice this. If not, draw their attention to it and explain why personification is a metaphor.

Daily log

Curriculum link: be taught technical terms such as metaphor

Purpose: for children to keep a personal reading, writing and thinking log in order to record thoughts and ideas for their own writing

- Ask the children to choose their best two metaphors rewritten to describe Grandad and write them in their Daily log. Make sure they orally rehearse each metaphor before they write it down.

Big Question

effective discussion; provide justifications for their views

Purpose: for children to develop their deeper thinking skills through a mini enquiry session based on a philosophical question relating to the work of the day

- Display today's Big Question on the **CD (file 5.2)**:

  If your class were an animal what would it be?

- Follow the process as explained at the end of Day 1 (p.48).

WRITING FICTION

DAY 6

Build an image – personification

using other similar writing as models for their own

Purpose: for children to be able to build a metaphor that can be used as the central image of a poem

- Say the line: 'The sea is a hungry dog.'
- Ask the children to TTYP to discuss what pictures this creates in their mind. Ask for feedback. Explain that the metaphor is personification of the sea – it says the sea has the qualities of a hungry dog.
- Repeat, subsituting different words for 'hungry' for example *The sea is an angry dog* and then *The sea is a lazy dog.*

- Now tell the children that you want to think of other ways of personifying the sea.

  TOL: Offer an idea for a different animal as a metaphor for the sea. For example, explain that when the sea crashes against the beach it could be said that it pounces like a cat or lion, so you could use the following metaphor: *The sea is a hunting lion.*

- Now ask the children to TTYP to share some ideas of their own about metaphors for the sea. As the children talk, listen for any original ideas and praise the children.

- Say the following line out loud and then ask children to repeat the line using MT/YT giving dramatic emphasis as you say it: *The sea is a hunting lion.*

  TOL: Explain that you are going to expand the line and create a more detailed picture. Explain that a hunting lion is very powerful like the sea and before it pounces it coils up just like a wave before it breaks, so the next line could be: *Powerful and coiled.*

- Click on the **CD (file 6.1)** to display the lines.

- Ask the children to say the lines using MT/YT.

Extend the metaphor

- TOL about what the sea does, i.e. the waves of the sea whirl, so you could say: *He whirls on the beach all day.*

- Ask the children if they think it would be possible to improve on the word *whirls*. Click on the **CD (file 6.2)** and display the line. Then click 'Synonyms' to show these words:

  tumbles   revolves   spins   swirls

- Re-read the line, substituting synonyms for whirls. Ask the children to show with thumbs up or down which ones they like. Tell the children that you like the word *tumbles*. Click 'New line' to show this new line:

  He tumbles on the beach all day.

- Tell the children that you are going to add to the metaphor of the sea as a lion. You will create an image of his eyes being fierce and black like a raging sea and of his tail being like the ever-moving waves.

- Click on the CD to show these new lines:

  He tumbles on the beach all day.
  With his fierce stormy eyes and swishing tail.

- Now ask the children, either individually or in pairs, to compose their own lines out loud using the Build a image – personification prompts in the Pupils' Book p.16. Do not let the children write until they can say their lines out loud. Once they have written them down, ask partners to take turns to develop each other's lines. Encourage crossings out, switching words round, etc. Emphasise that this is writing in action – it is not a neat, finished piece of writing!

Curriculum link: selecting the appropriate form

Build a form ⓒ🅓

Purpose: for children to think about how a poem is set out

- Remind the children that poetry that doesn't rhyme is called free verse and that the special term for writing that is not a poem is *prose*.

- Show the poem 'Mist' on the **CD (file 6.3)** and read it out loud using the line breaks to create pauses. TOL about how the poem is broken up into little phrases that give glimpses of the mist as it moves over the land.

- Draw the children's attention to the punctuation in the poem. It is two sentences! Click 'Sentences' and show the poem now as sentences. Explain that this is how it would be set out if it were in a story, i.e. if it were prose.

- Ask them to TTYP and each say one sentence. Ask them to discuss how reading the words as sentences has changed the feeling of the poem.

- Now navigate to the next screen and click 'Shape poem' to show the poem as concrete verse (a shape poem). Ask them to TTYP and read the poem and then discuss how the poem has changed now. What is emphasised? How do the shapes create images for them?

Daily log

Purpose: for children to experiment with different poetic forms

- Ask the children to experiment with different ways of organising the four lines they wrote about the sea. When they have created a form they could ask their partner to read it and discuss how they feel it has changed their lines.

Big Question

> Curriculum link: effective discussion; provide justifications for their views, distinguish between fact and opinion

Purpose: for children to develop their deeper thinking skills through a mini enquiry session based on a philosophical question relating to the work of the day

- Display today's Big Question on the **CD (file 6.4)**:

   Which is more powerful, the sea or the wind? *

- Follow the process as explained at the end of Day 1 (p.48).

* This Big Question will be revisited on Day 11 – the first day of the non-fiction week (p.60).

 DAY 7

> understand, through being shown, the skills and processes essential for writing

Build a poem 1

Purpose: for children to be able to see a poem grow through three stages of development

- Remind the children that they heard two versions of 'Rabbit in Mixer Survives' (Introducing the poem 1 & 2) before they heard and read the full poem. It prepared them to read the full poem.
- Tell the children that the poems about animals and the animal metaphor poems about the fog and the sea made another poet, Charlotte Raby, want to write about a water creature using water imagery and animal imagery.
- Display the image of a pike on the **CD (file 7.1)**. Remind the children of Ted Hughes' metaphor about the pike as a 'Robot shark', as well the way that he described the dark murky water that the pike lives in [see **CD (file 1.2)**]. Explain that Charlotte Raby used some questions to help her create the key images for her poem.
- Click 'Questions' to show the questions. Ask the children to TTYP and talk about their ideas for some of the questions before revealing the pre-prepared ideas for the poem by clicking 'Ideas'.
- Explain that you are going to show the children two versions of a new poem. This poem is based on the ideas generated from the picture of the pike. These versions prepared the writer to write the full poem.
- Now display Build a poem 1 on the **CD (file 7.2)**.
- Read the poem out loud to the children. Explain that you will soon show them another version of the new poem. This one has additional information and words – it has been developed.

> identifying how language, structure and presentation contribute to meaning

Build a poem 2

Purpose: for children to be able to see a poem grow through three stages of development

- Show Build a poem 2 on the **CD (file 7.3)**. TOL as you compare this version with Build a poem 1. Prepare your TOL before the lesson and click 'Highlights' to show highlighted examples of additional adjectives, information, alliteration and the expansion of a noun to a phrase.

Curriculum link:
understand,
through being
shown, the skills
and processes
essential for
writing

Build a poem 3

Purpose: for children to see an example of writing that will provide a model for their own writing

- Display **CD (file 7.4)**. Say that the poet used this as a skeleton to help her compose the final version of her poem. Explain that you are going to show them how the poet developed this poem into its final form. Use TOL as you annotate Build a poem 2 showing how it could be developed. Plan your TOL in advance.
- When you have modelled the writing, display **CD (file 7.5)** to show the final version of the poem. Remind the children that the Ted Hughes poem and the image of the pike inspired the poet, Charlotte Raby when she wrote this poem. Read the poem (Build a poem 3) to the children.

assessing the
effectiveness of
others' writing

Daily log

Purpose: for children to keep a personal reading, writing and thinking log in order to record thoughts and ideas for their own writing

- Ask the children to take turns to read a section each of Build a poem 3 printed from the **CD (file 7.6)**. Ask them to evaluate the poem by using the questions at the bottom of the sheet.
- Ask them to record their favourite poetic technique, line or idea from the poem in their Daily log.

effective
discussion; provide
justifications for
their views

Big Question

Purpose: for children to develop their deeper thinking skills through a mini enquiry session based on a philosophical question relating to the work of the day

- Display today's Big Question on the **CD (file 7.7)**:

  Why do we sometimes fear what we can't see?

- Follow the process as explained at the end of Day 1 (p.48).

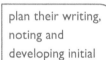

plan their writing,
noting and
developing initial
ideas

Write a poem 1

Purpose: to develop children's confidence and skills in poetry planning and development

- Before you start this activity print off copies of the sea creatures from the **CD (file 8.1)** so that the children can have their own copy of the sea creature they choose for their own poem.
- Tell the children that they are going to go through the stages of planning and rehearsing the poetic feature that they are going to use in their own poem, which is going to be about a sea creature.
- Display the Creatures of the deep slideshow on the **CD (file 8.1)**. Navigate through the screens, and pause so that you can TOL some responses and the children can TTYP and discuss the images that each picture brings to their minds.
- Remind the children that Charlotte Raby used questions to come up with the ideas for 'Pike in the deep'. Tell them that they should choose one of the sea creatures and make their brainstorm plan in their Daily log using the questions in the Write a poem 1 activity in the Pupils' Book p.17 to help them.

Write a poem 2

Purpose: for children to develop the poetic features of the poem

- Remind the children of the metaphor that was used in 'Pike in the deep'. It said the pike was a 'striped-lean-torpedo', a 'snapping water tiger' and used the simile that it was 'surgeon-like' when it cut through the water.

- Explain that you are going to focus on the imagery of the poem and practise metaphors for the whale shark (screen 3 of **CD [file 8.1]**). Display the metaphor *If the whale shark were a land animal it would be a cow* on the **CD (file 8.2)**.
- Remind the children that they used the metaphor game before to create imagery about Grandad Rabbit. Tell them they are going to TTYP and do the same for their sea creature by using the questions in the Pupils' Books p.18 (Write a poem 2, questions A to E). Take feedback.
- Display the Metaphor game on the **CD (file 8.3)** and explain that you are going to show the children how to extend the metaphor.
- Click on 'Extend' to display each metaphor. Use TOL to describe how they work.
- Now ask the children to look at the Write a poem 2 prompts in the Pupils' Book p.18 to create extended metaphors for their sea creature. Take feedback.

Curriculum link: using metaphors and similes

Daily log

Purpose: for children to keep a personal reading, writing and thinking log in order to record thoughts and ideas for their own writing

- Tell the children to choose two of their metaphors and turn them into similes. Remind them that they can say what their sea creature is *like* or they could use a noun and attach 'like' to the end of it, e.g. '*surgeon-like*' is used in 'Pike in the deep' to describe how the pike cut through the water.

effective discussion; provide justifications for their views

Big Question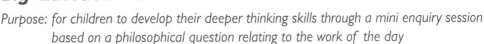

Purpose: for children to develop their deeper thinking skills through a mini enquiry session based on a philosophical question relating to the work of the day

- Display today's Big Question on the **CD (file 8.4)**:
  Can we call an animal a killer?
- Follow the process as explained at the end of Day 1 (p.48).

DAY 9

Write a poem 3

Purpose: for children to use the lines they have already developed to write their own poem

developing initial ideas

- Tell the children that they are ready to write their own free verse metaphor poem about a sea creature. Ask them to use the poetry writing Top Tips in the Pupils' Books p.19. Remind them to use any useful parts of the Anthology or their Daily log to help them and to look at the word wall for Power words and phrases and to use a thesaurus for synonyms.
- Encourage children to rehearse their ideas with their partners before they begin to write.
- Remind them to be willing to make changes and play with the sounds and rhythm of words as well as play around with the order of the stanzas and lines.

DAY 10

Read and share

Purpose: for children to read and share their poems

perform their own compositions

- Ask the children to read through their own poem.
- Now tell them to re-read their poem and underline their favourite parts. Ask them to share these with their partners. Collect feedback on best bits from partners.
- Make sure that any powerful words or phrases or vivid imagery are written on cards and added to the word wall.

<table>
<tr><td>

Curriculum link: assessing the effectiveness of their own and others' writing

</td><td>

Evaluate and edit

Purpose: for children to evaluate their own and their partner's work against specific criteria and then discuss how they could improve their work

- Display **CD (file 10.1)** to show the evaluation prompts and read them together using MT/YT.
- As a model, select an example of work from the children where the writing has met the criteria, and share this with the other children, explaining why it works well.
- Tell the children to take turns to read their partner's writing and discuss how well they have met the criteria.
- Ask children to discuss at least two changes they could make to improve their work following the partner discussion.

</td></tr>
</table>

proofread for spelling and punctuation errors

Proofread

Purpose: for children to proofread their work and make changes to improve the accuracy of their grammar, punctuation and spelling

- Now ask the children to proofread their work. If you have noticed that several children need to improve on a particular aspect of spelling, grammar or punctuation, use this as a focus for the Proofread activity. Write an example which includes common errors from the children's writing and use this as a model.
- The children should always be checking for standard use of punctuation and correct spelling of common exception words.
- The following points would be relevant as the particular focus for this Unit:
  - check for correct spelling of more ambitious vocabulary
  - check for correct use of punctuation for effect.

effective discussion; provide justifications for their views, distinguish between fact and opinion

Very Big Question

Purpose: for children to develop their willingness to broaden or revise their opinions through exploring one of the Big Questions in more depth

- See Unit 1 Day 10 for teaching notes on the Very Big Question (p.36).

Argument

In this non-fiction part of the Unit children will practise creating balanced arguments, as well as exploring how to organise a persuasive paragraph. 'Should humans *really* rule the Earth?' is a discursive argument text that explores whether or not animals might make a better job of looking after the planet. 'Animals Rule!…but which one?' is a series of persuasive paragraphs, which put across five animals' point of view as to why their species should rule the Earth.

See p.44 for the daily timetable for the Non-fiction week.

Non-fiction

Reading

Children will:

- understand the key features of argument texts and identify them
- understand the importance of pejorative and emotive language in argument texts
- analyse arguments to decide which is the strongest and give reasons for their answers.

Writing

Key writing purpose to be shared with the children:

To write an argument for a debate, persuading people to vote for the 'Animal Party'.

Writing evaluation to be shared with the children

My argument:

- is powerful and memorable, because I have used persuasive techniques such as pejorative and emotive language
- has a slogan, which sums up the main idea
- has an introduction and conclusion.

Grammar:

- uses layout devices to present information clearly for the reader.

See the Planning section of the Software ('Timetables' tab) for a printable version of the Writing purpose and evaluation.

Non-fiction: Argument

DAY 11

Curriculum link:
read and discuss
a range of
non-fiction

Linking the texts (CD)

Purpose: for children to make links between the story text and the non-fiction text

- Open **CD (file 6.4)** to display the Big Question from Day 6: *Which is more powerful, the sea or the wind?*
- Suggest that if the sea and wind were to discuss who was the most powerful that they would put across their point of view by giving evidence to back up their argument. They would try to prove that they were right.
- Ask the children to TTYP and discuss which points the wind might make to show that it was the most powerful. Choose some children to feed back.
- Explain that when you argue one point of view only (i.e. just the wind's), the argument is not balanced. You are not showing all the evidence. You are biased.
- Ask the children to TTYP and discuss what point the sea might make to show that it was the most powerful. Take feedback from the children.
- Now use this information to bring together a balanced argument such as: Some people believe that the wind is the most powerful force of nature because high winds such as tornadoes or hurricanes can pick up large objects such as houses. On the other hand many people believe that the sea is more powerful than the wind. This is because the sea erodes large objects like cliffs over time as well as washing away buildings if there is a tsunami.
- Explain that a balanced argument tries to show evidence for both sides and therefore offers the reader a chance to make up their mind.

exploring the meaning of words in context

Word power (CD)

Purpose: for children to become familiar with some words and synonyms associated with argument texts

> pejorative language   emotive language   logical   evidence   opinion

- Before the lesson, print all of the words and their definitions from the **CD (file 11.1)**.
- Show the words and definitions to the children and explain that they are words which will help us to identify and write argument texts.
- Display the words in sentences on the **CD (file 11.2)** and read them aloud to the children. Ask them to repeat using MT/YT.
- Display the words and definitions on your 'argument' word wall. Find opportunities to use the words yourself throughout the day, e.g. 'Where is the *evidence* for your *opinion*? Tell me the *facts*!' and encourage the children to use them in their everyday conversation.

identifying the audience for and purpose of the writing

Audience and purpose (CD)

Purpose: for children to understand how the introduction in an argument appeals to the audience and states its purpose

- Display and read aloud to the children the features of a good introduction to an argument on the **CD (file 11.3)**.
- Ask the children to read the introduction of 'Should humans *really* rule the Earth?' in the Anthology p.20 looking out for how well this argument begins. Tell them to TTYP and use the points in the Audience and purpose activity in the Pupils' Books p.20 to help them. Take feedback.

60

Curriculum link: Year 6 Grammar
punctuation of bullet points to list information, layout devices to structure text

Grammar: layout devices 🅰 Ⓒᴅ 🅿ᴮ

Purpose: to revise and develop children's ability to recognise and use a variety of layout devices to organise contents on the page. To develop children's awareness of the conventions of punctuation when using bullet points

- Tell the children to look at the presentation of the text 'Should humans *really* rule the Earth?' on pp.20–21 of the Anthology. Ask them to TTYP to describe the layout of the text on the page, e.g. numbered sections, columns, illustrations, bullet points.
- Collect feedback and make sure they have a secure understanding of what the term 'layout devices' means. Explain that there are other layout or presentational devices that can be used to organise different types of non-fiction texts to make the content appealing and easy to follow.
- Display **CD (file 11.4)** to show a list of layout devices. Read them aloud and then ask the children to TTYP to discuss and define the purpose of the first device listed: headings and subheadings. Choose two sets of partners to feed back and make sure that everyone agrees with the purpose of the device. Repeat the process with each of the listed layout devices.
- Click on 'Next' to show a section of the Anthology text. Ask the children to skim read the extract and TTYP to summarise the main points or ideas (keep this activity quite short). Choose two or three sets of partners to feed back.
- Explain that you have experimented with the organisation of the text using alternative layout devices. Click 'Next' to show the alternative layout.
- Ask the children to TTYP to identify the layout devices used and discuss whether they are an effective way of presenting the text, and why. Collect feedback from a few sets of partners to generate further discussion. You may wish to return to the previous slide to show the original extract for comparison.
- Remind the children that the layout devices used in the Anthology text included bullet points. Click 'Next' to show the bullet points from the Anthology text. Use the questions to help the children to identify the punctuation.
- Click 'Next' to show an alternative layout for the text. Explain how punctuation would be used if the bullets were combined to create one long sentence.
- Click 'Next' and read the text and the think bubble aloud. Discuss the effect of using each bullet to make a complete sentence.
- Now ask them to look at the Grammar: layout devices on p.20 of their Pupils' Book. Explain the activity and ask them to complete it with their partners. Choose two or three to share their answers. Clarify where necessary.

Homework Book p.10 provides further practice on layout devices.

noting ideas, provide justifications for their views

Daily log

Purpose: for children to keep a personal reading, writing and thinking log in order to record thoughts and ideas for their own writing

- Ask the children to think of three reasons why animals should be given the power to rule the Earth and to note these reasons in their Daily log.

 DAY 12

discuss and evaluate how authors use language

Deconstruction 1

Purpose: for children to understand how pejorative and emotive language creates a strong introduction for an argument

- Display the opening of the argument text 'Should humans really rule the Earth?' on the **CD (file 12.1)**. Read it aloud to the children using lots of expression so that the emotive and pejorative language really stands out.

- Remind the children that pejorative words create a negative connotation, for example if we say 'well-behaved children' we think of nice, happy children but if we say 'disciplined children' we might think of sad, silent children sitting in straight lines.
- Click 'Highlights' to highlight the pejorative language. TOL to explain how the first example makes you feel that human wars steal lives. The image created by the language is negative as it criticises humans for having wars.
- Ask the children to TTYP and discuss how each of the other pejorative phrases creates negative ideas or is critical. Ask the children to feed back their thoughts.
- Now click 'Highlights' again to show the emotive language. TOL to explain how the first example makes you feel – *famine, tyranny and terrorism makes me feel sad and scared; these are terrible things to be responsible for.*
- Ask the children to TTYP and discuss how each of the other emotive phrases makes them feel and why. Collect feedback.
- TOL to show how this introduction uses these emotional devices to set the tone of the argument. Ask the children to TTYP and discuss whether they think the writer's opinion shows in the introduction or not. Do they think the writer believes that animals should rule the Earth rather than man? Take feedback, encouraging the children to give evidence for their reasoning.

Read an argument

Curriculum link: identifying key details that support the main ideas

Purpose: for children to understand and locate examples of the key features of an argument text

- Display the Checklist for features of argument texts on the **CD (file 12.2)** and click 'Complete' to show the examples.
- TOL to explain the completed examples. Remind children that these words and phrases such as *however* and *on the other hand* help to make the steps of an argument clearer. Point out that 'Introduction' and 'Summary' have been left blank, as you want the children to summarise the key ideas in the next activity.
- Now hand out one between two copies of the empty grid printed from the **CD (file 12.3)**. Ask the children to work with their partners to complete their own grids using the whole of the 'Should humans *really* rule the Earth?' text in the Anthology pp.20–21. Take feedback.
- Explain to the children that this text will be used as a reference to help them to plan their own arguments, which will be slogans, leaflets and debate material to promote the Animal Party.

Daily log

noting ideas, evaluate how authors use language

Purpose: for children to keep a personal reading, writing and thinking log in order to record thoughts and ideas for their own writing

- Ask the children to choose five of the best emotive or pejorative phrases from the 'Should humans really rule the Earth?' text in the Anthology pp.20–21 and write them in their Daily log.

Scoring 'Animals rule!' – Deconstruction 2

Purpose: for children to understand how to structure a paragraph of an argument

using similar writing as models for their own

- Ask the children to take turns to read 'Animals rule' in the Anthology pp.22–23 with lots of expression to reinforce the argument each animal makes.
- Say that we are going to decide which animal made the best argument and to make it fair we are going to use the Scoring 'Animals rule' system in the Pupils' Book p.21 for each animal's argument.

- Model how to do this for the first animal using TOL to explain your marking. Now ask the children to work in pairs and mark the other animals. Take feedback and find out which animal is the winner.
- Display the paragraph plan on the **CD (file 13.1)**. Explain that this is a good way of organising your argument.
- TOL and scribe onto the plan how to plan an argument for the Animal Party:

My point of view is that animals are peaceful and therefore would not have wars. My evidence to support this is that animals don't have weapons. I will explain that unlike humans, animals do not own anything and so have no reason to fight.

- Ask the children to TTYP and use the paragraph plan to discuss what should be in a paragraph about how the Animal Party would educate children better than humans. Take feedback and scribe this on the CD.

Planning an argument

Purpose: for children to plan the main ideas and structure of their argument

Curriculum link:
plan their writing, noting and developing initial ideas

- Tell the children that they are going to focus on creating a plan for a debate saying why humans should vote for the Animal Party. Their argument needs to show the Human Party's point of view, but ultimately they need to persuade the audience to vote for the Animal Party (they are biased!).
- Display the 'Save our planet' advert on the **CD (file 13.2)** and ask the children to TTYP and discuss the slogan.
- Take feedback and discuss how 'Get on your bike!' sums up the main idea of the advert and tells the audience what to do.
- Ask the children to TTYP and discuss what the slogan for the Animal Party should be – what do they think its main idea should be and what do they want people to do? Take feedback.
- Tell the children to use Planning an argument in the Pupils' Books p.22. They should TTYP and plan a paragraph about how the Animal Party would look after the planet better than the Human Party. Invite the children to give their feedback.

Daily log

developing ideas, drawing on reading and research

Purpose: for children to keep a personal reading, writing and thinking log in order to record thoughts and ideas for their own writing

- Tell the children to read the posters 'People Power' and 'Animal Rule' in the Anthology p.23 and then have a go at composing a slogan for the Animal Party.

DAY 14

Deconstruction 3

Purpose: for children to practise composing sentences using words and phrases to structure arguments

evaluate how authors use language

- Tell the children that argument sentences use words and phrases that help create links between ideas and to explore cause and effect. Display Sentence 1 on the **CD (file 14.1)**.
- Drag and drop different examples into the sentence and TOL to explain how they change the meaning of the sentence slightly.
- Navigate to the next screen to show the next two sentences and repeat the process.
- Now ask the children to TTYP and compose a sentence about 'Animal Power' containing one of these words or phrases to structure their argument. Take feedback.

Curriculum link:
understand,
through being
shown, the skills
and processes
essential for
writing

Write debate materials

Purpose: for children to use their planning and notes to help them to write a draft of their argument

- Print off an Argument plan for each pair of children from the **CD (file 14.3)** so that they can use it later in this activity.
- Display the Argument plan on the **CD (file 14.2)**. Say that you are now planning an argument to convince humans to vote for the Animal Party.
- Remind the children how the introduction sets the tone of the argument. TOL through the introduction part of the plan modelling how you might plan the introduction.

  For example: I need a strong statement that draws the audience in, perhaps something like 'Humans have had their day, animals want the chance to put right human mistakes before it is too late'. My evidence could be a short list of human mistakes 1) Wars causing misery 2) Inequality where some people have too much when others are starving 3) Destruction of beautiful habitats. For the human point of view I'm going to use particular words or phrases to structure my argument 'On the other hand humans have made great achievements such as travel into space. However, we animals believe the cost of these achievements is too great!'

- Ask the children to TTYP and discuss what they might use in their introduction. Take feedback. Then ask the children to write their introduction on their plan.
- TOL the planning structure, highlighting the paragraph plans that they are already familiar with. Enter the headings on screen 4 to model how children could organise their paragraphs (*Education, Save our Planet* and *War*). Ask the children to TTYP and come up with key words/ideas for each point. Remind them to used pejorative and emotive language. Take feedback and then ask the children to write their ideas onto their planner.
- Now focus on the conclusion. TOL saying how important this is. It is the last thing the audience will hear. This is where their slogan should go!
- TOL using the prompts on the planner to sum up the Animal Party's arguments and remind the children to use pejorative language to show how badly humans have failed and emotive language to show how the Animal Party will do better. Ask the children to TTYP and discuss their conclusion. Take feedback. Then ask the children to write their conclusion onto their plan.
- Remind the children that there are Top Tips for organising an argument in the Planning an argument activity in the Pupils' Book p.22.
- Once the children have planned their argument give them time to edit and amend it, perhaps writing some parts more fully. Make sure they have time to practise saying their speech out loud with their partner and to work out who will say what!

proofread for
spelling and
punctuation errors

Proofread

Purpose: for children to proofread their work and make changes to improve the accuracy of their grammar, punctuation and spelling

- Now ask the children to proofread their work. If you have noticed that several children need to improve on a particular aspect of spelling, grammar or punctuation, use this as a focus for the Proofread activity. Write an example which includes common errors from the children's writing and use this as a model.
- The children should always be checking for standard use of punctuation and correct spelling of common exception words.
- The following points would be relevant as the particular focus for this Unit:
  - check that more ambitious vocabulary choices are spelled correctly
  - check that there is cohesion within a paragraph.

DAY 15

Curriculum link: presentations, provide reasoned justifications for their views

Present the argument PB

Purpose: for children to share their argument and to evaluate success

- Before the presentation give the children a final chance to practise their argument. Make sure they have shared out their speeches and have enough detail in their plans so that they can present a coherent argument.
- Tell them to read Writing an effective argument in their Pupils' Book p.22 and use the advice to improve their argument one final time.
- Invite another class to come and be the audience. Tell them that the Animal Party is coming to present their arguments and ideas for why they should rule the Earth rather than the humans.
- Let each pair present their argument. This should include their slogan, policy ideas and reasons why animals should rule rather than humans.
- At the end of the session ask the audience to vote on whether they want to be ruled by animals or humans.

assessing the effectiveness of their own and others' writing

Evaluate and edit CD

Purpose: for children to evaluate their own and their partner's work against specific criteria and then discuss how they could improve their work

- Display **CD (file 15.1)** to show the evaluation prompts and read them together using MT/YT.
- As a model, select an example of a presentation where the children met the criteria, and share with the other children why it worked well.
- Tell the children to discuss with their partner how well they met the criteria.
- Ask children to discuss at least two changes they could make to improve their presentation following the partner discussion.

perform their own compositions

Broadcast

- Now tell the children that they are each going to re-write their argument as an Animal Party TV broadcast. Tell them they will have one minute to get their point across and that they can use images, music and slogans to enhance their argument. Explain that they must think carefully about:
  - choosing the strongest arguments to focus on
  - making their point as succinctly as possible
  - how to appeal to the audience's emotions
  - which images, slogan and music would best support their presentation
  - how they are going to work as a group to present their broadcast.
- You may wish to video the broadcasts so that all the children can evaluate the success of their condensed argument. Invite the children to say what they thought worked well, whether the key messages were clear and if they were swayed by the content of the broadcast.

Fiction: Fiction genres
Non-fiction: Formal/impersonal writing

Timetable

WEEK 1 **Reading fiction**   *Brashem's tortoise*

Day 1	Day 2	Day 3	Day 4	Day 5
The story store	Think and link 1	Word power 2	Re-read a story version 3	What if not...?
Read a story version 1 📄	Word power 1 📄	Re-read a story version 3	Genre	Dramatic reconstruction 📄
Read a story version 2	Read a story version 3	Context	Daily log	Daily log
Respond and predict	Think and link 2	Daily log	Big Question	Big Question
Daily log	Daily log	Big Question		
Big Question	Big Question			

WEEK 2 **Writing fiction**   *Brashem's tortoise*

Day 6	Day 7	Day 8	Day 9	Day 10
Build a plan	Build a story 2	Similes and metaphor 📄	Write a story 3 📄	Share a story
Build a story 1	Build a story 3	Write a story 2		Evaluate and edit
Daily log	Evaluation 📄	Daily log		Proofread
Big Question	Write a story 1 📄	Big Question		Very Big Question
	Daily log			
	Big Question			

WEEK 3 **Reading and writing non-fiction**   *Formal/impersonal writing*

Day 11	Day 12	Day 13	Day 14	Day 15
Introduction	Word power 2 📄	Deconstruction 2 📄	Dramatic reconstruction	Persuasive presentations 📄
Word power 1 📄	Deconstruction 1	Grammar: formal writing	Daily log	Evaluate and edit
Prefixes	Write a formal/ impersonal text 1	Write a formal/ impersonal text 2		
Grammar: passive and active voice	Daily log *	Proofread		
Grammar: formal/ impersonal speech and writing		Daily log		
Daily log				

📄: shows that a file should be printed out from the Software.

* you will need some examples of formal/impersonal writing for this activity

Overview of the Unit

The short story *Brashem's Tortoise* has been chosen for its use of small domestic detail to evoke a past era. Set in 1938, the story provides an historical setting that is accessible and easily connected to children's own experiences. The children use this text and extracts from others to explore key features of a variety of fiction genres. They work in role to explore stock characters and settings and focus on different methods of planning for effective writing.

In the non-fiction part of the Unit children are introduced to the key features of impersonal/formal writing. They examine the audience and purpose of texts about exotic animals and animal smuggling and how spoken language can be adapted to suit a different purpose and audience. For more information about the Non-fiction week and the Non-fiction writing evaluation criteria, see p.79.

The Homework Book provides a homework activity related to the content of this Unit for each of the three weeks.

Fiction

Reading

Children will:

- think about the different genres of fiction writing, e.g. *fantasy, adventure, horror*
- focus on the genre of historical writing, and look for details that Susan Price describes in *Brashem's Tortoise* to show that it is set in the 1930s
- empathise with the characters through drama and by learning more about the historical context of the story.

Writing

Key writing purpose to be shared with the children:

To write a story in a genre of my choice, using powerful imagery to build a picture of the setting in the reader's mind.

Writing evaluation to be shared with the children

My story:

- uses features typical of my chosen genre
- creates powerful and unusual images using simile, metaphor and personification
- uses a combination of narrator's voice and dialogue to move the story along.

See the Planning section of the Software ('Timetables' tab) for a printable version of the Writing purpose and evaluation.

Fiction: Fiction genres
Brashem's Tortoise by Susan Price

READING FICTION

DAY 1

Curriculum link: read and discuss an increasingly wide range of fiction

Resources
PB Pupils' Book, pp.23–34
A Anthology, pp.24–39
CD CD on interactive whiteboard (Unit 3)
GB Grammar Bank on CD
HB Homework Book, pp.11–13

The story store (CD)

Purpose: for children to revise their understanding of the term 'fiction genres'

- Tell the children that the word genre is a French word meaning types of... or kinds of... Explain that the word fiction means made-up stories. Say the phrase *fiction genres* and its definition: fiction genres means types of made up stories. Use MT/YT (My turn/Your turn) to allow the children to articulate the phrase.
- Now tell the children that there are many different fiction genres and that some are easily recognised and categorised, while others could slide about between a few categories.
- Use the **CD (file 1.1)** to show book blurbs for Mary Shelley's *Frankenstein*, Lewis Carroll's *Alice in Wonderland* and R.L. Stevenson's *Treasure Island*. Explain that these stories represent the genres of fantasy, adventure and horror.
- Read the blurbs out loud to the children and ask them to TTYP (Turn to your partner) to discuss which genre they would match to which story. Collect feedback from the children asking for reasons for their choices. Avoid going into too much detail about different genres at this stage, stick to the obvious features.
- Tell the children they are now going to hear the bare bones of another story which is from a different genre. It is a story about two mischievous girls who play a trick on a shop keeper to get what they want and we are going to call it Story version 1.

Read a story version 1 (CD)

Purpose: for children to become familiar with Story version 1, the bare bones of the story Brashem's Tortoise

- Read Story version 1 aloud all the way through to the children. (Do not reveal any surprises or the ending of the final story.)
  Story version 1
  1. A girl and her friend find someone's pet tortoise.
  2. They return it to its owner.
  3. The owner gives them a reward.
  4. They are thrilled.
  5. They have a plan to get more rewards.
  6. It involves playing a trick on the pet's owner.
  7. The plan is put into action several times and it works.
  8. Something goes wrong with the plan and they have to face the consequences.
- Use MT/YT and TTYP for each point. This is to help the children to hold the basic story in their heads. Now display Story version 1 on the **CD (file 1.2)**.

predicting; identifying how language, structure, and presentation contribute to meaning

Read a story version 2 (CD)

Purpose: for children to examine how Story version 2 provides additional information for the reader and for children to become more familiar with the story before they hear the full version

- Read Story version 2 aloud to the children.

Story version 2

1. A girl called Jessie and her friend Olive find a shopkeeper's pet tortoise.
2. They go to the grocery shop to return it to its owner, Mrs Brashem.
3. The shop is dark with lots of smells. It is the front room of Mrs Brashem's house.
4. Mrs Brashem rewards them with something from her shop.
5. They are thrilled because they hardly ever get any treats. It is 1938 and times are hard.
6. Jessie and Olive have a plan to get more rewards.
7. The plan involves taking something from Mrs Brashem and playing a trick on her.
8. The plan works so they do it again several more times, but then things go wrong.
9. They get caught out and they have to make amends.

- Re-read the text, stopping after each section to ask the children if there are any words that tell them more about the people and the story. TTYP and feed back.
- Now display this version on the **CD (file 1.3)**. Click on the 'Highlights' icon to identify the additional information.
    - We know the names of the main characters – Jessie, Olive and Mrs Brashem.
    - Addition of the information that the tortoise owner has a grocery shop that is actually the front room of her house.
    - Description of the shop as dark with lots of smells.
    - Addition of the information that the girls hardly ever get any treats.
    - Addition of the fact that it is 1938 and that times are hard.
    - Addition of the fact that the girls take something from Mrs Brashem.
    - We know that Jessie and Olive have to make amends for their actions.
- TOL and use TTYP to share how this extra information changes the pictures in our head as we hear the story.

Respond and predict

Purpose: for children to use their personal response to the story so far to predict how the story might develop and end

> **Curriculum link:** checking that the story makes sense to them, predict

- Ask the children to TTYP and use the Respond and predict questions in the Pupils' Book p.23 to discuss their personal responses to the story so far and to predict possible developments and endings.
- Collect feedback and encourage the children to give rationales for their ideas.

Daily log

Purpose: for children to be introduced to the process of keeping a personal log of notes, thoughts and ideas, collected from their reading and discussions, to use in their own writing

- See notes in Unit 1 (p.24). Explain to the children that they are going to continue to collect thoughts and ideas in their Daily log.
- Ask the children to record the definition of *genre* in their Daily log and which language the word comes from.

Big Question   (CD)

> effective discussion; provide justifications for their views

Purpose: for children to develop their skills of argument and discussion through a mini enquiry session based on a philosophical question relating to the work of the day

- Display today's Big Question on the **CD (file 1.4)** and remind the children that the shopkeeper in the story has a pet tortoise:

Tortoises are classed as exotic animals and some species are now endangered. Should humans be allowed to have exotic animals as pets? *

* This Big Question will be revisited on Day 11 – the first day of the non-fiction week (p.80)

- Ask the children to TTYP to discuss. Collect feedback from partners and scribe some responses using the CD writing tool. Tell the children that each day's Big Question and their thoughts on paper will be put in a safe place until the end of week 2. They will then vote on which question to discuss more deeply. See Introduction for further notes (p.13).

DAY 2

Curriculum link: identifying themes

Think and link 1 (CD)

Purpose: for children to make links and connections with a particular genre

- Display the **CD (file 2.1)** to show Story version 2 and a list of genres. Ask the children to think about what they know about the story so far and to TTYP to discuss any clues as to which genre it might turn out to be. They might pick up on the old-fashioned names of the children, the date mentioned, the fact that 'times were hard' or the description of the grocery shop.
- Collect feedback and encourage further discussion and explanation of choices.

exploring the meaning of words in context

Word power 1 (CD)

Purpose: for children to develop their knowledge and application of rarer vocabulary and synonyms based on words taken from the text

> scuttled   lurked   reek   luscious   grimacing   snivelled

- Tell the children that the writer Susan Price has used some powerful verbs and adjectives in the story and these are words that are not commonly used in everyday conversations.
- Display the list of words and their definitions in Word power 1 on the **CD (file 2.2)**. Look at the words with the children and then read the sentences to them. Ask the children to repeat the sentences using MT/YT, giving dramatic emphasis and actions as you say them.
- Find opportunities to use the words yourself during the day e.g. 'I *scuttled* across the car park in the rain today like a little beetle!' Encourage the children to use the words at home with friends and family so that they become embedded in their own spoken, and eventually written, vocabulary.
- Print the words and their definitions from the **CD (file 2.3)** and display on your word wall.
- Now tell the children to do the Word power 1 activity in the Pupils' Book p.24.

explain and discuss their understanding of what they have read

Read a story version 3 🄰 🄿🄱

Purpose: for children to hear and enjoy the full version of the story for the first time

- Tell the children they are now going to hear the whole story for the very first time. Show your enthusiasm before you start. TOL about which parts you can't wait to hear about, etc.
- Read the full story from the Anthology p.24 to the children. Read with great enjoyment and use appropriate intonation and body language to add to your storytelling performance!
- At the end of the story, ask the children to TTYP to discuss the Read a story version 3 questions in the Pupils' Book p.24. Collect feedback.

Think and link 2

Purpose: for children to make links and connections with a particular genre

- Ask the children to TTYP to discuss whether they have changed their opinion about the genre of *Brashem's Tortoise* now that they have heard the full story.
- Collect feedback and explain that it is an historical genre text.
- Explain that this genre can mean that a) it was written a long time ago in the past or b) it was written recently but set a long time ago in the past.
- Ask the children to TTYP to decide whether *Brashem's Tortoise* is a) or b). Collect feedback and clarify where necessary, selecting parts of the text from the Anthology to verify the answer (b) e.g. where the narrator tells the reader that 'A parrot wouldn't be allowed in a shop selling food these days' (p.25) or 'The shop wasn't like a modern shop' (p.25).

> **Curriculum link:** summarising the main ideas

Daily log ⓒⒹ

Purpose: for children to keep a personal reading, writing and thinking log in order to record thoughts and ideas for their own writing

- Ask the children to create a mind map of the story *Brashem's Tortoise* in their Daily log. You may wish to display Story version 2 again on the **CD (file 2.4)** to support them. Encourage them to add in any extra details they can remember or that they found interesting from the full story reading. Suggest some categories for the mind map 'branches' and write them on the board to help them.

> effective discussion; provide justifications for their views

Big Question ⓒⒹ

Purpose: for children to think about and discuss a philosophical question relating to the work of the day

- Display today's Big Question on the **CD (file 2.5)**:

  Can children be wiser than adults?

- Follow the process as explained at the end of Day 1 (p.70).

> **DAY 3**

Word power 2 ⓒⒹ

Purpose: for children to increase their knowledge and understanding of old fashioned or little used words from the text

> exploring the meaning of words in context

carbolic soap   button-hooks   wash-boards   cooking-range   blacklead

- Tell the children that there are some words in the story that are old-fashioned words, usually the names of the things we don't use nowadays.
- Explain that it is important that we know what these words mean if we want to create pictures in our minds as we hear or read the text.
- Display the **CD (file 3.1)** to show the words and the explanations. Read them out loud and ask the children to repeat them using MT/YT.

> checking that the story makes sense to them

Re-read a story version 3

Purpose: for children to gain a deeper understanding of the story

- Let the children follow their own copy of the text in their Anthology p.24 as you re-read the full version of the story aloud with great enthusiasm. Stop at the Power words in bold so that the children can jump in. (*See introduction for further explanation.*)
- Now ask the children to read their copy of the story with their partners, each alternating reading the sections, and to read the words and phrases in bold with great expression to show understanding. Explain that you will be listening in.

Curriculum link:
identifying key details

Context (CD)

Purpose: for children to understand the historical context of the story

- Remind the children that *Brashem's Tortoise* is set in 1938 and that means it is written in an historical genre.
- Display the short PowerPoint presentation on the **CD (file 3.2)** about what life was like for children living in Britain in 1938. Click 'Audio' to play the audio for each image.
- Play it a second time and ask the children to make notes in their Daily log about what they consider to be the most important and/or interesting points.
- Ask them to TTYP to share their feelings about the differences between their own lives and the lives of children living in the 1930s.
- Collect feedback and encourage discussion about what they think Jessie and Olive's lives would have been like.
- Tell the children to find out if there are people in their family who grew up in the 1930s and to record what they find in their Daily log. Encourage them to bring in a relevant photograph to be scanned and printed and pasted in their Daily log.

noting ideas, provide reasoned justifications for their views

Daily log

Purpose: for children to keep a personal reading, writing and thinking log in order to record thoughts and ideas for their own writing

- Tell the children to identify, in their opinion, at least two positive and two negative things about life in the 1930s.
- Ask them to write them down in their Daily log and then share their lists with their partner.

effective discussion; provide justifications for their views

Big Question (CD)

Purpose: for children to think about and discuss a philosophical question relating to the work of the day

- Display today's Big Question on the **CD (file 3.3)**:

  Have inventions such as TV, the Internet and mobile phones made our lives better or worse?

- Follow the process as explained at the end of Day 1 (p.70).

DAY 4

read silently

Re-read a story version 3

Purpose: for children to deepen their understanding of a story by increasing familiarity with the text

- Ask the children to read the whole story from the Anthology p.24 silently. Tell them that they can stop to record any thoughts, ideas, questions and favourite bits in their Daily log as they read the text. Explain that it is more important for them to think about what they are reading than to finish first and, as they know the story already, it doesn't matter if they don't finish this time.

identifying and discussing themes and conventions in and across a range of writing

Genre (CD) (PB)

Purpose: for children to be able to identify and comment on the key features of a variety of genres

- Display the **CD (file 4.1)** to show the genre grid. Click 'Complete' to reveal the 'typical features' of historical texts and explain these to the children. Ask the children to TTYP to locate examples of the features in the text *Brashem's Tortoise* to link it to the historical genre.

- Collect feedback and add some of their answers in the 'Examples from the text' cells.
- Now remind the children of the blurb they looked at for the three stories and their identified genres. Click 'Complete' to reveal the features of the next genre, i.e. horror/supernatural.
- Ask the children to TTYP to share what they know about the story of Frankenstein. Add basic information/examples of features, e.g. Frankenstein's monster, stormy night, monster made of body parts from the dead, etc. Repeat for the other two genres using the blurb on the **CD (file 1.1)** as a guide.
- Now ask the children to look at the extracts from different fiction texts in the Pupils' Book p.25 and follow the prompts to identify the genres they represent. Collect feedback and add some of their answers and examples in the empty cells of the **CD (file 4.1)** genre grid.

Curriculum link: provide reasoned justifications for their views

Daily log

Purpose: for children to keep a personal reading, writing and thinking log in order to record thoughts and ideas for their own writing

- Ask the children to TTYP to discuss their favourite genre of book or film. Ask them to record in their Daily log their choices along with examples of actual books or films they have read or watched in that genre.

effective discussion; provide justifications for their views

Big Question

Purpose: for children to develop their skills of argument and discussion through a mini enquiry session based on a philosophical question relating to the work of the day

- Display today's Big Question on the **CD (file 4.2)**:

  Why do we like to frighten ourselves with horror stories and films?

- Follow the process as explained at the end of Day 1 (p.70).

DAY 5

drawing inferences and justifying, identifying key details

What if not...?

Purpose: for children to explore how characters, settings and events are represented in particular genres

- Ask the children to look at the What if not...? question in the Pupils' Book p.26.
- Tell the children to TTYP and discuss this using the prompt questions as a guide. Collect feedback and encourage others to build upon ideas. Give your opinion too.

identifying themes and conventions

Dramatic reconstruction

Purpose: for children to become familiar with a scenario that could be used later for writing

- Organise the children into groups of four or six. Give each set of partners a copy of the genre/scenario planning sheets printed from the **CD (file 5.1)**.
- Tell the children that each group will use the planning sheets to improvise a short play in a particular genre. Explain that you have 'borrowed' elements of the historical story *Brashem's Tortoise* and used them in the different genres.
- Ask them to choose one genre and scenario from the sheets and then plan their play to include features of the genre using the information to guide them. (You may prefer to select the genres for the children to avoid duplication.)
- Give the children enough time to plan and rehearse their plays. Tell them that each group is going to perform their plays to the rest of the class in turn.
- After each performance ask the children to TTYP to discuss which genre they thought the scene was representing and what clues they used to work this out.

Curriculum link: assessing the effectiveness of others' writing

Daily log

Purpose: for children to keep a personal reading, writing and thinking log in order to record thoughts and ideas for their own writing

- Ask the children to TTYP to discuss which of the plays they watched they thought was the most interesting or effective and why. Tell them to record their opinions in their Daily log.

effective discussion; provide justifications for their views

Big Question

Purpose: for children to develop their skills of argument and discussion through a mini enquiry session based on a philosophical question relating to the work of the day

- Display today's Big Question on the **CD (file 5.2)**:

  Is pretending only for little children?

- Follow the process as explained at the end of Day 1 (p.70).

WRITING FICTION

 DAY 6

plan their writing

Build a plan PB

Purpose: for children to understand that there are different methods of planning a story quickly and effectively

- Tell the children that you had an idea for a new story and you want to share with them how the seed of the idea started, grew and developed into a plan.
- Explain that first of all you made a few notes in your own Daily log. Display the **CD (file 6.1)** to show a page of rough notes and ideas.
- Tell the children that there are lots of ways of using basic notes to plan a story. Say that sometimes you use story graphs to plan your stories. Display the **CD (file 6.2)** to show the example of a story graph. Click to show the speech bubbles and use them to talk through how the notes have been used with the graphs.
- Explain that sometimes you prefer to use a planning grid. Display the **CD (file 6.3)** to show how the grid has been filled in using prompts from the Daily log notes.
- Now ask the children to look at the story graph and the notes about *Brashem's Tortoise* in the Pupils' Book p.26. Tell them to TTYP to discuss the order and the possible answers to the questions referring to the story in the Anthology p.24.
- Collect feedback and encourage argument and different opinions supported by valid reasoning.

plan their writing by using other similar writing as models for their own

Build a story 1

Purpose: for children to be able to see a story grow through three stages of development

- Remind the children that they heard two versions of *Brashem's Tortoise* (Story versions 1 and 2) before they heard and read the full story. It prepared them to read the full story.
- Tell them that you are going to show them two versions of the new story to be written based on the idea of the boys and the poisoned fish. Take the role of writer for these activites. Explain that these versions helped you to write the full story – they are another way of planning and then developing a story. Show the Build a story 1 questions on the **CD (file 6.4)** and explain that these were the prompts that helped you to know what to put in the new story.
- Now display Build a story 1 on the **CD (file 6.5)** and read each point out loud to the children.

Daily log

Purpose: for children to keep a personal reading, writing and thinking log in order to record thoughts and ideas for their own writing

- Ask the children to TTYP to discuss what genre the new story is most likely to be. Tell them to write what they think along with reasons in their Daily log.

 effective discussion; provide justifications for their views

Big Question CD

Purpose: for children to develop their skills of argument and discussion through a mini enquiry session based on a philosophical question relating to the work of the day

- Display today's Big Question on the **CD (file 6.6)**:

  How do we know if a story is fact or fiction – real or made up?

- Follow the process as explained at the end of Day 1 (p.70).

(DAY 7)

Build a story 2 CD

understand the skills and processes essential for writing

Purpose: for children to be able to see a story grow through three stages of development

- Remind the children that they looked at your Build a story 1 yesterday. Show Build a Story 2 on the **CD (file 7.1)**. TOL as you compare this version with Build a story 1. Click 'Highlights' to show additional information, synonyms and adjectives, and talk about how these change the pictures in our mind.

using similar writing as models for their own

Build a story 3 CD

Purpose: for children to see an example of writing that will provide a model for their own writing

- An example story is provided as a model for writing. Remain in the role of the writer of this story during these activities.
- Tell the children that you have written a first draft of the story (Build a story 3). Display the story on the **CD (file 7.2)**. Explain that when writing this story your purpose was to entertain, excite and interest the audience or reader.
- Read the story to the children.

assessing the effectiveness of others' writing

Evaluation CD 🖨 PB

Purpose: for children to develop their ability to evaluate the effectiveness of a piece of writing

- Tell the children that you know this first draft of the story needs improving. Give out copies of printouts of the story from **CD (file 7.3)**. Ask the children to TTYP to read alternate paragraphs of the story together and then TTYP to give an immediate, personal response to the story. Collect feedback.
- Now ask the children to evaluate the writing more formally using the guide questions in Build a story 3 in the Pupils' Book p.28. Collect feedback and encourage discussion and constructive criticism.

plan their writing, noting and developing initial ideas

Write a story 1 CD 🖨

Purpose: for children to be able to plan and draft a story in a particular genre

- Give each child a copy of Choose a genre printed from the **CD (file 7.4)**. Explain that the story ideas are similar to the scenarios they used for their improvised plays on Day 5, p.73.
- Explain that they are each going to draft a story in a genre of their choice using genre information and story ideas from the sheet.
- Give the children time to look at the Choose a genre sheet and to decide which one they want to use for their story writing. They do not have to choose the same genre they used for their drama work on Day 5.

- Ask them to TTYP to discuss the reasons for their choices. Collect feedback.
- Make sure the children understand that the story ideas are just suggestions. Encourage them to make as many changes to the story ideas given on the sheet as they wish, but they must make sure the changes fit the features of their chosen genre.
- Now tell the children to use any of the methods they know (e.g. a mind map, Story 1, 2, 3, story graph, story planning grid) to start planning their own story. Remind them to use any parts of their Daily log they think might be useful.
- Tell the children that they will have some of the next day's lesson to complete their plans.

Curriculum link: noting ideas, provide reasoned justifications for their views

Daily log

Purpose: for children to keep a personal reading, writing and thinking log in order to record thoughts and ideas for their own writing

- Tell the children what the term *working title* means. Ask the children to share ideas for one or two working titles for their story that are in keeping with their chosen genre. Ask them to record their ideas in their Daily log and explain why they think it is a good title.

effective discussion; provide justifications for their views

Big Question

Purpose: for children to develop their skills of argument and discussion through a mini enquiry session based on a philosophical question relating to the work of the day

- Display today's Big Question on the **CD (file 7.5)**:

  Should you always forgive someone who does something wrong?

- Follow the process as explained at the end of Day 1 (p.70).

(**DAY 8**)

Similares and metaphor

Purpose: for children to explore examples of simile, metaphor and personification as a model for their own writing

pupils should be taught the technical and other terms needed for discussing what they hear and read, such as metaphor and simile

- Tell the children that as they develop their story, you want them to think about using similes and metaphors to enrich their work.
- Explain that Susan Price creates powerful and unusual pictures in our heads through her use of similes and metaphor in *Brashem's Tortoise* and these can help them to think of their own similes and metaphors.
- Tell them that she also uses personification (when something that is not alive is given the qualities of something that is alive) when she is describing Brashem's shop. Ask the children to look in the Anthology p.24 and read the sentence beginning 'When you opened the door...'.
- Display the **CD (file 8.1)** to show the examples of similes and metaphor in *Brashem's Tortoise*.
- Go through the examples drawing out why they are effective and reminding the children of the difference between similes and metaphors. Add some ideas for your own similes and metaphors into the boxes.
- Give each child a printout of the **CD (file 8.2)** and ask them to add their own similes and metaphors in the empty boxes.
- Ask them to TTYP to share their examples. Collect feedback/examples to share with the group.
- Now ask the children to make sure they have at least two similes and one metaphor ready to use in the completed version of the story they are going to be developing. Tell them that if they want an extra challenge, they could add one example of personification!

Write a story 2 (CD)

Purpose: for children to be able to organise their ideas into a cohesive opening paragraph

Curriculum link: using similar writing as models for their own, writing narratives

- Tell the children that they are going to continue to work on their plan for a story in a particular genre. Remind them to use any parts of their Daily log to help them.
- Walk around as the children work noting interesting ideas, clear plans and good examples of genre features.
- When they have had long enough to complete their plans, give feedback on what you noted as you walked round.
- Tell them that you have had a go at writing the opening paragraph for one of the genres. Display the **CD (file 8.3)** to show the paragraph and use your own ideas and/or the speech bubbles to talk about the writing process and genre features. The paragraph is split over two screens.
- Now tell the children that they are ready to use their plans to help them to write the first draft of an opening paragraph for one of the three genres. Explain that they can change and edit their draft as they write each sentence and paragraph or get their ideas down on paper and then edit them afterwards. Remind them that whichever method they use, they must keep re-reading what they have written to check it makes sense.

Daily log

draft and write by selecting appropriate vocabulary, understanding how such choices can change and enhance meaning

Purpose: for children to keep a personal reading, writing and thinking log in order to record thoughts and ideas for their own writing

- Ask the children to read through what they have written today. Tell them to find more interesting or powerful synonyms for at least two words in their text.
- Tell them to record their original words and one or more synonyms in their Daily log. They can then edit their actual texts if they are happy that the synonym is appropriate and improves the writing.

Big Question (CD)

effective discussion; provide justifications for their views

Purpose: for children to develop their skills of argument and discussion through a mini enquiry session based on a philosophical question relating to the work of the day

- Display today's Big Question on the **CD (file 8.4)**:

  Can we choose what type of person we are?

- Follow the process as explained at the end of Day 1 (p.70).

DAY 9 — Write a story 3 (CD)

Purpose: for children to experiment with words and phrases to create cohesion between paragraphs to help them to structure a story

writing narratives, using devices to build cohesion within and across paragraphs

- Tell the children that they will have most of the lesson to continue writing and editing/re-drafting their stories in their chosen genre.
- Explain that as they add more paragraphs, they need to think about the structure of the story as a whole.
- Tell them that writers often use particular words and phrases to end or begin a new paragraph. They are like the links that hold the structure together. Explain that different kinds of links can change the structure and feel of a story.
- Display the **CD (file 9.1)** to show some examples and talk through the effect for the reader, e.g. the narrator can share what they know with the reader, they can signal movement in time (either backwards or forwards), they can create strong emotions in the reader when they know something a character doesn't know yet.

- Now tell the children to try to include one of these ways of varying the structure of their story as they work on the next few paragraphs.
- You may wish to display the cohesive words and phrases which can be printed from the **CD (file 9.2)**.

DAY 10

Share a story

Curriculum link: assessing the effectiveness of their own and others' writing

Purpose: for children to be able to look critically at their writing

- Ask the children to read through their own stories, underlining their favourite parts. Ask them to share these with their partners. Collect feedback on best bits from partners.
- Make sure that any powerful or unusual words or phrases used are added to the word wall.
- Ask the children to think about which character they would most like to be from their own story. Tell them to TTYP to discuss their choices and reasons.

Evaluate and edit ⓒ

Purpose: for children to evaluate their own and their partner's work against specific criteria and then discuss how they could improve their work

- Display **CD (file 10.1)** to show the evaluation prompts and read them together using MT/YT.
- As a model, select an example of work from the children where the writing has met the criteria, and share this with the other children, explaining why it works well.
- Tell the children to take turns to read their partner's writing and discuss how well they have met the criteria.
- Ask children to discuss at least two changes they could make to improve their work following the partner discussion.

Proofread

proofread for spelling and punctuation errors

Purpose: for children to proofread their work and make changes to improve the accuracy of their grammar, punctuation and spelling

- Now ask the children to proofread their work. If you have noticed that several children need to improve on a particular aspect of spelling, grammar or punctuation, use this as a focus for the Proofread activity. Write an example which includes common errors from the children's writing and use this as a model.
- The children should always be checking for standard use of punctuation and correct spelling of common exception words.
- The following points would be relevant as the particular focus for this Unit:
  - check speech has been punctuated correctly
  - check for correct use of punctuation for effect, e.g. ellipsis and exclamation marks
  - check for correct spelling of more ambitious vocabulary choices
  - check for consistent use of tense.

Very Big Question

effective discussion; provide justifications for their views, distinguish between fact and opinion

Purpose: for children to develop their willingness to broaden or revise their opinions through exploring one of the Big Questions in more depth

- See Unit 1 Day 10 for teaching notes on the Very Big Question p.36.

Formal/impersonal writing

READING AND WRITING NON-FICTION

In the non-fiction part of the Unit children study examples of impersonal/formal writing. They write short examples of formal/impersonal texts. The children plan and enact a role-play based on an encounter between a customs officer and someone they suspect is trying to smuggle exotic animals for the pet market.

See p.66 for the daily timetable for the Non-fiction week.

Non-fiction

Reading

Children will:

- read a range of formal/impersonal writing to find out more about keeping exotic pets
- understand the key features of formal/impersonal writing and identify them in texts
- identify the passive and active voice.

Writing

Key writing purpose to be shared with the children:

To plan and rehearse a role-play based on an encounter between a customs officer and an exotic pet smuggler, with appropriate use of formal and informal language.

Writing evaluation to be shared with the children

Our role-play:

- includes ideas from our storyboard to structure the dialogue so it has a beginning, middle and end
- uses a formal/impersonal style for the customs officer including official language, e.g. *It is not permitted…*, *in accordance with…*
- uses informal, personal language for the smuggler.

Grammar:

- uses the passive and active voice correctly and consistently.

See the Planning section of the Software ('Timetables' tab) for a printable version of the Writing purpose and evaluation.

Curriculum link: learn the conventions of different types of writing

Introduction

Purpose: for children to develop their understanding of formal/impersonal writing using the context of one of the Big Questions and the fiction text studied in weeks 1 and 2

- Show the Big Question from Day 1 on the **CD (file 1.4)**: *Tortoises are classed as exotic animals and some species are now endangered. Should humans be allowed to have exotic animals as pets?*
- Ask the children to TTYP to recall some of the thoughts and ideas they had in their discussion. Collect feedback.
- Remind the children that in the story *Brashem's Tortoise*, Mrs Brashem kept two exotic animals as pets – a parrot and a tortoise.
- Now remind them that the story was set in 1938 and attitudes about importing animals from the wild for the UK pet market were very different then. Explain that there were fewer laws as well so it is unlikely that Mrs Brashem would have known or perhaps even thought about how the animals had been captured, kept and imported before she bought them.
- Tell the children that there are now many rules, regulations and laws about importing, selling and buying exotic animals and these are recorded in texts that use formal and impersonal language suitable for a particular audience and purpose.
- Explain that during the week, they will be looking at information about exotic pets, but first they need to understand some of the features of formal/impersonal writing.

exploring the meaning of words in context

Word power 1

Purpose: for children to become familiar with some words and synonyms associated with formal/impersonal writing

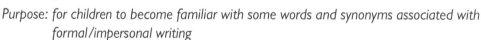

| present | impersonal | formal | official | passive |

- Display the words and definitions on the **CD (file 11.1)**. Explain that they are words that will help us to identify and write formal/impersonal texts. Read each word and sentence to the children. Ask the children to repeat the sentences using MT/YT.
- Print out the words and definitions from the **CD (file 11.2)** and display on your 'formal/impersonal' word wall. Find opportunities to use the words yourself during the day, e.g. "Let's do it now – there's no time like the *present!*" and encourage the children to use them in their everyday conversation.
- Now tell the children to do the Word power 1 activity in the Pupils' Book p.29.

use prefixes

Prefixes

Purpose: for children to revise how prefixes change the meanings of root words

- Tell the children that we can add a prefix to many words and change the meaning of the word. Explain that there are lots of different prefixes and the more we read, the more likely we are to remember which ones to use with which root words.
- Display the **CD (file 11.3)** to show the root word and prefixes grid.
- Click on the 'Reveal' icon to display the prefixes and the changed meaning of the root words.
- Ask the children to TTYP to see if they can work out what the meaning of the prefixes *im*, *in* and *un* from the chart. What do they have in common?
- Collect feedback and praise thoughtful and interesting suggestions. Make sure they know that they are all ways of indicating what something is *not*.
- Tell the children that they are known as negative prefixes. Now click on the 'Prefixes' icon to display this information.

Curriculum link: Year 6 Grammar
use of the passive voice to affect the presentation of information in a sentence

Grammar: passive and active voice (CD) (PB)

Purpose: for children to develop an awareness of the active and the passive voice and how it affects presentation of information

- Remind the children that all sentences contain a *subject* and an *object*, e.g. **Jake** patted the dog. The focus is on the *subject* **Jake** who is carrying out the action shown by the *past tense verb* **patted** (the dog). The dog is being affected by or receiving the action carried out by Jake. The **dog** is the *object*.
- Display **CD (file 11.4)** to show the sentence with the subject and verb colour coded. Explain that this sentence is written in what is called the *active voice* and it is the voice we use most often in both our speaking and our writing because it sounds natural. Use the think bubbles to explain and reinforce the children's understanding of the concept.
- Click 'Next' to show the same sentence written in the *passive* voice instead. Use MT/YT to read the sentence out loud. Use the think bubbles to explain that the focus has moved away from Jake, to the dog – the dog has become the subject.
- Say that the passive voice sounds much less natural and is often used in formal, impersonal speech and writing than informal, personal speech and writing.
- Use MT/YT to read the first of sentences below. Ask the children to TTYP to discuss whether it is written in the active or passive voice and to give their answer chorally. Then click 'Next' on the CD file to show the sentence and the answer. Clarify using the think bubble. Then click 'Next' to show the sentence written in the passive voice instead. Repeat the process for each sentence:
  - The children are riding bikes.
  - The cabbages were eaten by the rabbit!
  - The letter will be delivered by the postman.
  - Auntie Jasbir climbed the mountain for her favourite charity.
- Tell the children that sentences spoken or written in the passive voice can sometimes leave out information about who or what is doing the action, leaving us with a less clear understanding of what exactly is happening, has happened or will be happening.
- Click on 'Next' to show examples based on the same sentences. Use MT/YT to read each sentence and then ask the children to TTYP to discuss why leaving out information about who or what is doing the action might be a useful device. Choose two or three sets of partners to share their ideas, e.g. it might not be important to know that information; the speaker or writer might not want us to know who or what is responsible for the action, such as in a mystery story.
- Now ask them to look at the Grammar: passive and active voice activity on p.30 of their Pupils' Book. Explain the activity and ask them to complete it with their partners. Choose two or three sets of partners to share their answers and clarify where necessary.

Year 6 Grammar
the difference between the structures typical of informal speech and structures appropriate for formal speech and writing, use of the subjunctive

Grammar: formal/impersonal speech and writing (PB)

Purpose: for children to be able to recognise the basic features of formal/impersonal writing and to introduce the children to examples of the subjunctive in very formal speech and writing

- Tell the children that depending on the audience and purpose of the text, the writer might use any or all of lots of different features of formal/impersonal writing.
- Display the **CD (file 11.5)** to show some common language features of these text types.
- Use your own ideas and click 'TOL' to explain the features more fully. Navigate to the next slide and repeat.

Non-fiction: Formal/impersonal writing

- Now display the **CD (file 11.6)** to show extracts from three formal texts and a features grid. Talk through the given examples of features from text A.
- Click on 'Next' to display texts B and C and use TOL and TTYP to complete the grid with the children. Scribe children's reponses onto the grid.
- Now ask the children to TTYP to try to put in their own words what effect this kind of writing has on the reader, e.g. power of the message is in the straightforward, unemotional facts and figures rather than emotive language, writing seems unbiased (even if it isn't) because the writer is anonymous, formal language makes it sound serious and important, etc.
- Make sure the children's ideas are valued even if they are not quite accurate or articulated clearly – this is a challenging task! Clarify and secure a basic understanding of the effect of impersonal/formal writing on the reader.

Subjunctive

- Tell the children that in informal speech and writing we would normally use the verb *was* in the verb phrase *If I was…* This would be in a sentence that expresses an idea about possibilities or wishes. Use MT/YT to say the sentence below and then write it on the board or a flipchart.

  If I was a better singer, I would be happy to perform.

  Underline the verb *was*. Say that the same idea about a possibility or wish could be presented in a much less usual, very formal way. Use MT/YT to say the sentence *If I were a better singer, I'd be happy to perform*.

- Write it on the board or a flipchart. Underline the word *were* and say that this form of the verb *was* is used when a much more formal way of speaking or writing is required. Explain that some people believe that it is more poetic and is better at expressing the mood of *what is not*, rather than *what is*: wishes and possibilities.
- Say that another example of using the subjunctive would be when we want to use a verb to indicate that something has to/must be done.
- Write the sentence *The teacher insists that Abigail play the piano every day* on the board or flipchart and underline the verb *plays*. Explain that in the more formal version, the verb loses the -s ending. Write this sentence on the board, underline the verb *play* and use MT/YT to say the sentence.
- Now ask the children to look at the Grammar: formal/impersonal speech and writing activity on p.31 of their Pupils' Book. Explain the activity and ask them to complete it orally with their partners. Choose two or three to share their sentences and clarify the meaning of the original sentences where necessary.

Homework Book pp.13–14 provide further practice on formal/impersonal writing and speech.

Curriculum link: recognising vocabulary and structures that are appropriate for formal speech and writing

Daily log

Purpose: for children to keep a personal reading, writing and thinking log to record thoughts and ideas for their own writing

- Ask the children to choose at least one example of the formal impersonal sentences in their Pupils' Book and then re-write it in their own words, using less formal language.
- Tell them to TTYP to share their written versions and to discuss whether they are less or more effective than the originals, and why.
- Choose two or three to share a written sentence then ask them for feedback from their discussion about its effectiveness.

DAY 12

Curriculum link: exploring the meaning of words in context

Word power 2

Purpose: for children to increase their knowledge of rarer words and their synonyms

> *exotic   confinement   trafficking   lobbying*

- Display the words and definitions on the **CD (file 12.1)**. Explain that they are words that they need to know the meaning of before they read some formal/impersonal texts in the Anthology.
- Read each word and sentence to the children. Ask the children to repeat the sentences using MT/YT.
- Print out the words and definitions from the **CD (file 12.2)** and display them on your word wall.

using similar writing as models for their own

Deconstruction 1

Purpose: for children to read and analyse a text that provides a model for impersonal/formal writing

- Ask the children to find the printed web pages about *Exotic Pets* in the Anthology p.34. Explain that these are good examples of formal/impersonal writing about an interesting topic – the selling, buying and keeping of exotic animals as pets.
- Tell them to take turns to read a section of the texts on pp.34–37 aloud using expression and intonation to show understanding.
- Now ask them to TTYP to share their first thoughts about the exotic pet trade. Collect feedback and use their contributions as an opportunity to clarify the purpose of the text.
- Display the **CD (file 12.3)** to show a short extract from a text in the Anthology. Navigate to the second screeen and click 'Reveal' to show examples of the key features of formal/impersonal writing.
- Explain that these features help the writer to organise a lot of information and make important points clearly and concisely. Tell the children that they are going to find out how effectively the writer of the Exotic Pets web pages has done this, by trying to locate key information quickly and accurately.
- Ask the children to look at the Deconstruction 1 activity in the Pupils' Book p.32 and TTYP to follow the prompts and questions.
- Remind them to make written notes as they find answers to the questions.
- Now ask the children to discuss with their partners the things that helped them to be able locate the information needed to answer the questions.
- Collect feedback and refer back to key features that might have helped, e.g. impersonal tone and so lack of emotive language and unnecessary information; structured layout with bullet points and sub-heading; clear statements of facts supported by statistics; written in present tense all the way through which makes the information seem timeless (not something that has already happened) and current.

summarising the main ideas

Write a formal/impersonal text 1

Purpose: for children to develop their ability to retrieve and record key information. To summarise the information, using features of formal/impersonal writing

- Tell the children that an important skill is to be able to pick out the most important points of a text and summarise it in a shortened form.
- Tell them that the Exotic Pets text in the Anthology pp.36–37 has over 300 words altogether and that they are going to write a summary of what it tells us about exotic pets and the exotic pet trade from their reading and understanding of the text, using no more than 150 words.

- Display the **CD (file 12.4)** and explain that this is a short extract from a different text about global warming that has some of the features of formal/impersonal writing, e.g. it is written in the present tense, it is written in an impersonal voice, it has a formal vocabulary.
- Read the extract out loud to the children and then use your own ideas and/ or click 'TOL' to show the speech bubbles to help you to model the process of selecting and summarising key information from a text.
- Now ask the children to re-read the text again from the Anthology pp.36–37 and to make notes on the key points they want to include from the different sections.
- Tell them to TTYP to share their notes and see if they have picked the same points to include and to revise their notes if they think it is necessary.
- Now ask the children to write the first draft of their summary, re-reading what they have written after every sentence to see if they can edit out any words without losing meaning. Remind them to try to sustain the impersonal voice and present tense in their summaries.
- Remind them that this is not intended to be a polished piece of writing – it is an opportunity to practise sifting information and present it in a formal/impersonal, concise form.
- Walk around as the children are working on their summaries, noting points to clarify and selecting examples to use as exemplars in feedback.

> **Curriculum link:** retrieve and record information from non-fiction

Daily log

Purpose: for children to keep a personal reading, writing and thinking log in order to record thoughts and ideas for their own writing

- Tell the children that over the next few days, you want them to look in magazines, newspapers, junk mail or packaging for examples of formal/impersonal writing of any kind. Give them some examples that you have found already, such as forms, certificates, official letters, competition rules, games rules, etc.
- Ask them to bring them to school to stick in their Daily log. Tell the children to write a note next to each one of where they found it.

> **DAY 13**

> identifying the audience for and purpose of the writing, identifying key details

Deconstruction 2

Purpose: for children to be able to identify the audience and purpose of a text and to evaluate the importance of information in a text

- Tell the children to look at the text in the Anthology pp.38–39. Explain that this is another web page about exotic pets.
- Read the text out loud to the children, reminding them of any Word power 2 vocabulary and synonyms on the word wall, and explaining any other tricky words.
- Ask them to TTYP to discuss what they think the purpose and target audience of the text is. Collect feedback and encourage the children to find examples from the text to support their answers.
- Display the **CD (file 13.1)** of a mind map template and give each child a printed copy of their own. Explain that they are going to use the template to help them to create a mind map to show what they think are the most important points made in the web page for PEPS (Protection of Exotic Pets Society).
- Guide the children through the process of selection and recording using the completed examples.
- Ask the children to re-read the text silently by themselves before creating their own mind maps using the template to help them.

- Walk around and question children about their choices as they work. Note good examples of selection, based on appraisal of its importance, to praise and share in your feedback to the class.
- Tell the children that most of the text on pp.38–39 is also written in an impersonal/formal style but there are certain parts that have a slightly more personal and informal tone.
- Ask them to TTYP to discuss and identify these parts of the text. Collect feedback and encourage further explanation of choices and discussion.

Grammar: formal writing A ⓒⒹ

Purpose: for children to be aware of the style and syntax of particular phrases typical of very formal, official documents

> *valid for the aforementioned*
>
> *in accordance with*
>
> *prohibited and punishable by law*

- Tell the children to find the part of the text on pp.38–39 in the Anthology that mentions 'official documentation'. Ask them to TTYP to come up with a definition of what the phrase means. Collect feedback and clarify where necessary.
- Write the word on a card and put it on your formal/impersonal word wall.
- Ask the children to TTYP to recall different examples of official documents – they may want to check their Daily log for the samples they found at the end of Day 12 (see above).
- Collect feedback and make a generic list, e.g. driving licence, parking ticket, birth certificate, will, laws, rules, etc.
- Display the **CD (file 13.2)** to show three more phrases often found in official documents. Read them and their definitions out loud and use MT/YT for just the phrases to encourage the children to become more confident when saying rarer or technical words and phrases.
- Explain that lots of special phrases can be found in official documents. They are usually written in the most formal/impersonal style of all texts.

Homework Book p.13 provides further practice on formal and informal writing.

Write a formal/impersonal text 2 ⓒⒹ 🅿️

Purpose: for children to see examples of formal documentation and to use it as a model for their own writing

- Display the **CD (file 13.3)** to show some extracts from official documents with special phrases highlighted. Ask the children to TTYP to discuss what the extracts mean. Then click 'Reveal' to show the extracts re-written in a personal/informal style. Ask the children to compare them with the original extracts written in an impersonal/formal style.
- Talk through the differences, emphasising the different styles and features, such as more frequent use of complex sentences in the formal/impersonal style extracts. Encourage the children to TTYP to suggest reasons why the impersonal/formal style is used for official documentation.
- Now tell the children to look at the Write a formal/impersonal text activity in the Pupils' Book p.33 and to read the extract from an official document (a law about keeping dangerous dogs) written in an inappropriately personal/informal style.

Curriculum link: Year 6 Grammar formal writing

developing ideas, using similar writing as models for their own

- Ask them to TTYP to discuss why it doesn't sound right or appropriate for an official document. Collect feedback from the children.
- Now tell the children to re-write the extract using an impersonal/formal style of writing.
- Remind them to think of more formal synonyms for certain words.
- Remind them to try to include a complex sentence.

Proofread

Purpose: for children to proofread their work and make changes to improve the accuracy of their grammar, punctuation and spelling

Curriculum link: proofread for spelling and punctuation errors

- Now ask the children to proofread their work. If you have noticed that several children need to improve on a particular aspect of spelling, grammar or punctuation, use this as a focus for the Proofread activity. Write an example which includes common errors from the children's writing and use this as a model.
- The children should always be checking for standard use of punctuation and correct spelling of common exception words.
- The following points would be relevant as the particular focus for this Unit:
  - check the spelling of official language, e.g. permitted, prosecuted and license
  - check the structure of complex sentences.

Daily log

Purpose: for children to keep a personal reading, writing and thinking log in order to record thoughts and ideas for their own writing

retrieve and record information from non-fiction, drawing on research

- Ask the children to TTYP and go on the Internet and/or to the library and do a bit of detective work to find out about the real Dangerous Dogs Act. When did it become law? Why? Which dogs are classed as dangerous? (You may need to approach this topic with care as it could be a sensitive subject.)
- Tell them to record their findings in their Daily log.

DAY 14

Dramatic reconstruction

Purpose: for children to develop their understanding of how spoken language is adapted to suit a different purpose and audience

recognising vocabulary and structures that are appropriate for formal speech and writing

- Tell the children that the exotic pets texts in the Anthology mention the role of customs officers. Ask the children to TTYP to discuss what they already know about what a customs officer's role is. Collect feedback and scribe correct suggestions on the board. Clarify further if necessary.
- Display the **CD (file 14.1)** to show a short comic strip about a customs officer's encounter with a suspicious character. Click 'Audio' to listen to the audio for the comic strip on each screen.
- Talk through the differences between the formal/impersonal speech of customs officer Kate and the jewellery smuggler.
- Ask the children to TTYP to discuss why the language and style of Kate's think bubbles is different to her speech bubbles. Collect feedback.
- Display the **CD (file 14.2)** to show some real life photos of animals that were trying to be smuggled. Ask the children to TTYP to see if they can work out what is being smuggled in each one. Take feedback.
- Tell the children that they are going to plan and rehearse a short role-play based on an encounter between a customs officer and someone s/he suspects is trying to smuggle an exotic animal for the pet market.

- Tell the children to look at the Dramatic reconstruction activity in the Pupils' Book p.34 and to follow the Top Tips to help them to create their role-plays.
- Allow the rest of the lesson for planning and rehearsing their role-plays.

Daily log

Purpose: for children to keep a personal reading, writing and thinking log in order to record thoughts and ideas for their own writing

- Ask the children to TTYP to discuss whether they ever change they way they speak, e.g. in front of their grandparents, their friends, strangers.
- Tell them to record their answer in brief note form.

 DAY 15

Curriculum link: perform their own compositions

Persuasive presentations

Purpose: for children to complete and present their role-plays and to evaluate each other's work

- Allow fifteen minutes for the children to practise their role-plays.
- Divide the class into groups. There should be four sets of partners per group.
- Organise the children so that each set of partners has an opportunity to a) perform in front of other sets of partners b) watch at least three other performances.
- Depending on the size and ability of your group you may need to use another lesson to complete the performances.

assessing the effectiveness of their own and others' compositions

Evaluate and edit

Purpose: for children to evaluate their own and their partner's work against specific criteria and then discuss how they could improve their work

- Display **CD (file 15.1)** to show the evaluation prompts and read them together using MT/YT.
- As a model, select an example of a role-play where the children met the criteria, and share with the other children why it worked well.
- Tell the children to discuss with their partner how well they met the criteria.
- Ask children to discuss at least two changes they could make to improve their presentation following the partner discussion.

Fiction: Stories with flashbacks
Non-fiction: Biography and autobiography

Timetable

WEEK 1 **Reading fiction** *Gone Away!*

Day 1	Day 2	Day 3	Day 4	Day 5
The story store	Word power 1 📄	Word power 2 📄	Grammar: formal and informal vocabulary	What if not...?
Read a story version 1	Respond and predict	Re-read a story version 3	Re read a story version 3	Dramatic reconstruction 🖨
Think and link 1	Read a story version 3	Moods and feelings	Flashbacks	Daily log
Read a story version 2	Daily log	Daily log	Daily log	Big Question
Daily log	Big Question	Big Question	Big Question	
Big Question				

WEEK 2 **Writing fiction** *Gone Away!*

Day 6	Day 7	Day 8	Day 9	Day 10
Build a beginning	Build a story 1	Write a story 1	Write a story 3 🖨 *	Share a story
Tell a story	Build a story 2	Write a story 2		Evaluate and edit
Daily log	Build a story 3	Daily log		Proofread
Big Question	Evaluation 🖨	Big Question		Very Big Question
	Daily log			
	Big Question			

* Scissors are required for each child

WEEK 3 **Reading and writing non-fiction** Biography and autobiography

Day 11	Day 12	Day 13	Day 14	Day 15
Introduction	Think and link	Write a biography 1	Write a biography 3	Biography presentations
Biographical writing	Word power 🖨	Deconstruction 2	Proofread	Evaluate and edit
Your research 🖨	Deconstruction 1	Write a biography 2	Daily log	Write an autobiography 🖨
Daily log	Daily log	Daily log		

🖨: shows that a file should be printed out from the Software.

Overview of the Unit

Lou Kuenzler's story *Gone Away!* uses economical but evocative language and flashbacks to explore friendship, loss and guilt. Children will experiment with these techniques in their own writing.

The linked non-fiction work is based on biographical and autobiographical reading and writing with opportunities for children to present work in electronic form and participate in peer evaluations.

Please note that the text *Gone Away!* explores the potentially sensitive subject of bereavement and this should be taken into account in particular teaching circumstances. For more information about the Non-fiction week and the Non-fiction writing evaluation criteria, see p.102.

The Homework Book provides a homework activity related to the content of this Unit for each of the three weeks.

Fiction

Reading

Children will:

- understand how flashback is used in *Gone Away!* to recreate past events and reveal more about Brendan and Leon's friendship
- identify the different moods and feelings the author has created in the story
- use role-play to explore alternative scenarios for the story.

Writing

Key writing purpose to be shared with the children:

To write a new short story with flashbacks, based on Gone Away!

Writing evaluation to be shared with the children

My story:

- uses time signals (backwards and forwards) to signal to the reader when things happen
- develops thoughts and feelings in the new episode that are appropriate to the characters of Leon and Brendan
- uses dialogue which sounds appropriate to the characters, and tells us something new about their friendship

Grammar:

- includes dialogue which is punctuated correctly.

See the Planning section of the Software ('Timetables' tab) for a printable version of the Writing purpose and evaluation.

Fiction: Stories with flashbacks
Gone Away! by Lou Kuenzler

READING FICTION

Resources
PB Pupils' Book, pp.35–42
A Anthology, pp.40–53
CD CD on interactive whiteboard (Unit 4)
GB Grammar Bank on CD
HB Homework Book, pp.14–16

DAY 1

Curriculum link:
identifying and discussing themes and conventions, making comparisons across stories

The story store (CD)

Purpose: for children to develop an understanding of different story structures

- Tell the children that many written stories and films reveal events through a device known as *flashback*. Explain that using flashback is a way of revisiting and recreating people, times and places that have gone forever – the writer can transport a character and a reader to the past and back to the present again.
- Use the **CD (file 1.1)** to show the summaries of *Robinson Crusoe* by Daniel Defoe and *Kensuke's Kingdom* by Michael Morpurgo which both use flashbacks as a narrative device. Explain that even though they were written hundreds of years apart, both of these stories explore the themes of loss and friendship through flashback.
- Read the summaries out loud to the children.
- Tell the children they are now going to hear the bare bones of another story that uses flashback. It is a story about a boy who has mixed feelings about a lost friend and we are going to call it Story version 1.

Read a story version 1

Purpose: for children to become familiar with Story version 1, the bare bones of the short story Gone Away! by Lou Kuenzler

- Read Story version 1 aloud all the way through to the children. (Do not reveal any surprises or the ending.)
  Story version 1
  1. A boy's friend has left.
  2. The friend's family have moved house.
  3. The boy is asked to visit.
  4. He looks back at their friendship.
  5. The boy makes a new friend and they get on well.
  6. He compares the old and the new friend.
  7. The boy starts to face some uncomfortable truths.
  8. A visit takes place.
- Use MT/YT (My turn/Your turn) and TTYP (Turn to your partner) for each point. This is to help the children hold the basic story in their heads.

Think and link 1 (CD)

making comparisons

Purpose: for children to make links and connections with other stories and their own experiences

- Display Story version 1 on the **CD (file 1.2)**. TOL about it, asking yourself and answering questions about your own experiences of friendship and circumstances that change, etc. Use TTYP to encourage the children to link their experiences in the same way.
- Return to the Story store summaries **CD (file 1.1)** and ask the children to TTYP to discuss how they might link to Story version 1 apart from the flashback device. Collect feedback.

Curriculum link:
predicting;
identifying
how language
and structure
contribute to
meaning

Read a story version 2

Purpose: for children to examine how Story version 2 provides additional information for the reader and for children to become more familiar with the story before they hear the full version

- Read Story version 2 to the children.
  Story version 2
  1. Leon's best friend, Brendan, has gone away.
  2. Brendan's family have moved house for a new beginning.
  3. Leon is invited to visit the family at their new home.
  4. He reminisces about his relationship with Brendan.
  5. Leon makes a new friend called Sam. They get on well and like the same things.
  6. Leon compares his time spent with Brendan and Sam and gets confused about how he feels.
  7. Gradually, Leon starts to confront some awkward truths.
  8. A visit occurs and a change takes place.
- Re-read it, stopping after each section to ask the children if there are any words that tell them more about the people and the story. TTYP and feedback.
- Now display this version on the **CD (file 1.3)**. Click 'Highlights' to identify the additional information
  - Addition of the adjective *best* to describe Leon's friend.
  - Addition of the information that Brendan's family want *a new beginning*.
  - Addition of the fact that Leon and Sam like the same things.
  - Addition of the information that Leon *gets confused* when he compares Sam to Brendan.
  - Addition of the adverb *gradually* to describe how Leon confronts awkward truths.
  - Addition of the fact that *a change takes place* after a visit takes place.
  - We know some of the characters' names – *Leon, Brendan* and *Sam*.
- TOL and use TTYP to share how this extra information changes the pictures in our minds as we hear the story.

Daily log

Purpose: for children to be introduced to the process of keeping a personal log of notes, thoughts and ideas, collected from their reading and discussions, to use in their own writing

- See the notes in Unit 1 (p.24). Explain that they are going to continue to collect thoughts and ideas in their Daily log.
- Ask the children to TTYP to discuss what they would miss most about their lives if they were stranded on a desert island and to record their thoughts in their Daily log.

Big Question

Purpose: for children to develop their skills of argument and discussion through a mini enquiry session based on a philosophical question relating to the work of the day

- Display today's Big Question on the **CD (file 1.4)**.

  Can we ever really know what living in the past was like? *

  * This Big Question will be revisited on Day 11 – the first day of the non-fiction week (p.103)

- Ask the children to TTYP to discuss. Collect feedback from partners and scribe some responses. Tell the children that each day's Big Question and their thoughts will be put in a safe place until the end of Week 2. They will then vote on which question to discuss more deeply. See Introduction for further notes (p.13)

DAY 2

Curriculum link:
exploring the meaning of words in context

Word power 1

Purpose: for children to increase their knowledge of and application of synonyms and to examine how writers use language for effect

> left   gone away   looks back   reminisces
> uncomfortable   awkward   takes place   occurs

- Tell the children that there are some words in Story version 2 that are synonyms for words in Story version 1.
- Display Story version 1 and Story version 2 on the **CD (file 2.1)** and click 'Synonyms' to identify the synonyms – *left/gone away, looks back/reminisces, uncomfortable/awkward, takes place/occurs.*
- TOL and use TTYP to share an example of how some of these words change the pictures in our minds as we hear the story. Ask the children to TTYP to discuss other examples.
- Print all of these words and their synonyms from the **CD (file 2.2)** and display them on your word wall.
- Try to use some of these words during the day where appropriate, pointing them out on your word wall as you say them.

checking the story makes sense to them, predicting what might happen

Respond and predict 🔲

Purpose: for children to use their personal response to the story so far to predict how the story develops and ends

- Ask the children to TTYP and use the Respond and predict questions in the Pupils' Book p.35 to discuss their personal responses to the story so far and to predict possible developments and the ending.
- Collect feedback and encourage the children to give rationales for their ideas.

explain and discuss their understanding of what they have read

Read a story version 3 🔲 🔲

Purpose: for children to hear and enjoy the full version of the story for the first time

- Tell the children they are now going to hear the whole story for the very first time. Show your enthusiasm before you start. TOL about which parts you can't wait to hear about, etc.
- Read the full story from the Anthology p.40 with great enjoyment to the children. Use appropriate intonation and body language to add to your story telling performance.
- At the end of the story, ask the children to TTYP to discuss the Story version 3 questions in the Pupils' Book p.35. Then collect feedback.

making comparisons

Daily log

Purpose: for children to develop their thinking and recording skills by logging their initial response to the whole story

- Tell the children that now they know the full story they can compare how the story developed with the predictions they made about the story with their partner.
- Ask the children to record in their Daily log which parts of the whole story surprised them and which parts (if any) matched their own predictions.

effective discussion; provide justifications for their views

Big Question

Purpose: for children to develop their skills of argument and discussion through a mini enquiry session based on a philosophical question relating to the work of the day

- Display today's Big Question on the **CD (file 2.3)**:

  Can we change other people or only ourselves?

- Follow the process as explained at the end of Day 1 (p.91).

DAY 3

Curriculum link:
exploring the meaning of words in context

Word power 2

Purpose: for children to develop their knowledge of and application of rarer vocabulary taken from the text; for children to understand how writers use language for effect

| *hoarse* | *nonchalant* | *vengeful* | *manipulative* | *forlorn* |

- Tell the children that the writer of the story *Gone Away!* has used a mixture of informal, everyday spoken language and words and phrases that are not commonly used in everyday conversations.
- Display the Word power 2 words and their definitions from the **CD (file 3.1)**. Look at the words with the children and then read the sentences to them. Ask the children to repeat the sentences using MT/YT giving dramatic emphasis and actions as you all say them.
- Find opportunities to use the words yourself during the day, e.g. 'No, we can't have P.E. today and it's no use trying to *manipulate* me!' Encourage the children to use the words at home with friends and family so that they become embedded in their own spoken (and eventually, written) vocabulary.
- Print all of these words and their definitions from the **CD (file 3.2)** and display them on your word wall.

checking that the story makes sense to them

Re-read a story version 3 🅰

Purpose: for children to gain a deeper understanding of the story and to see the text for the first time

- Let the children follow their own copy of the text in their Anthology p.40 as you re-read the full version of the story aloud with great enthusiasm. Stop at the Power words in bold so that the children can jump in. (*See introduction for further explanation.*)
- Now ask the children to read their copy of the story with their partners, alternating reading each section, and to read the words and phrases in bold with great expression to show understanding. Explain that you will be listening in.

discuss and evaluate how authors use language

Moods and feelings 🅰 🅿🅱

Purpose: for children to be able to identify and comment on the mood and feelings conveyed in a text

- Tell the children that a good writer can create emotional responses in a reader by creating different moods and feelings in a text.
- Ask the children to TTYP to discuss what moods and feelings they think are created in the story *Gone Away!*, for example *gloomy, hopeful, upsetting, confused*. Encourage them to skim read parts of the text in their Anthology p.40 to identify a wider range of emotions than the most obvious ones.
- Now ask them to write in their Daily logs single words or phrases to describe the different feelings and moods they have identified.
- Collect feedback and scribe their words and phrases on the board or on card to put on your word wall. Encourage them to think of synonyms for generic terms such as *sad, happy, nice* that they might offer.
- Tell the children to TTYP and use the Moods and feelings questions in the Pupils' Book p.36 and the notes they made in their Daily log to explore where the writer created these moods and feelings. Take feedback.

Fiction: Stories with flashbacks

Curriculum link: learning new vocabulary

Daily log

Purpose: for children to keep a personal reading, writing and thinking log in order to record thoughts and ideas for their own writing

- Ask the children to start collecting words and their synonyms that describe different moods.
- Tell them to make a chart with different levels of words to describe the same mood, e.g.

sad	unhappy	upset	distraught
happy	pleased	delighted	ecstatic
cross	annoyed	angry	furious

effective discussion; provide justifications for their views

Big Question

Purpose: for children to develop their skills of argument and discussion through a mini enquiry session based on a philosophical question relating to the work of the day

- Display today's Big Question on the **CD (file 3.3)**:

  If you feel guilty about something, does it mean that you are?

- Follow the process as explained at the end of Day 1 (p.91).

DAY 4

Grammar: formal and informal vocabulary

Purpose: for children to revise and deepen their understanding of the differences between formal and informal vocabulary in speech and writing. To increase their awareness of when one might be more appropriate than the other

Year 6 Grammar the difference between vocabulary typical of informal speech and vocabulary appropriate for formal speech and writing

- Ask the children to look at the first section of the story *Gone Away!* on p.40 of their Anthology and to TTYP to discuss who is narrating the story and how they know. Choose two sets of partners to share their answers, making sure they can identify the narrator as Leon and that it is written in the first person.
- Say that the writer has had to 'catch' the voice and language of a young boy, Leon, to make the narration convincing and appropriate. Ask the children to TTYP to discuss whether the vocabulary and style of language in the opening section is formal or informal. Collect feedback and ask for examples from the opening of the text to support their ideas.
- Display **CD (file 4.1)** to show some informal phrases taken from the text and ask the children to TTYP to think of more formal vocabulary as replacements for the words that are underlined. You may need to prompt the children by giving a few suggestions to start with. Choose two or three sets of partners to feed back.
- Use MT/YT to say some of their examples. Scribe some of their ideas in the editable text box. You may wish to offer rarer, very formal examples of your own.
- Remind the children that there are often occasions when we need to be able to use more formal vocabulary in speech or writing. Say that you have some examples to show them and they are going to see if they can identify in which situation each of them might be heard or read.
- Click 'Next' to show the first example. Read it out chorally with the children. Ask them to choose the most likely situation from the list shown and to Popcorn their answer. Choose two children to explain their choice. Click through the slides and repeat the process for the next two examples.
- Now ask them to look at the Grammar: formal and informal vocabulary activity on p.37 of their Pupils' Book. Explain the activity, ask them to complete it with their partners orally. Now tell them to create two columns, one headed 'Formal' and

the other headed 'Informal' and then to write the words that are shown in bold in their Daily log under the appropriate headings.
- Read each word aloud and ask the children to give the answer formal or informal chorally. Check their understanding and clarify if necessary.
- Remind them that formal vocabulary is not necessarily better than informal vocabulary. Make sure they understand that we have to learn when one is more appropriate or effective than the other.

Homework Book p.14 provides further practice on formal and informal vocabulary.

Curriculum link: read silently

Re-read a story version 3 🅰

Purpose: for children to deepen their understanding of a story by increasing familiarity with the text

- Ask the children to read the whole *Gone Away!* story silently from the Anthology p.40. Tell them that they can stop as they read the text to record any thoughts, ideas, questions or favourite bits in their Daily log. Explain that it is more important for them to think about what they are reading than to finish first and, as they already know the story, it doesn't matter if they don't finish this time.

identifying how language and structure contribute to meaning

Flashbacks 🆑

Purpose: for children to be able to identify and comment on the use of flashback to reveal layers of emotions and meanings in a text

- Explain to the children that recalling the past usually evokes a mixture of emotions:

  Recollection of happy times – happy memories but sad that they are over.

  Recollection of sad times – sad memories but happy that they are over.

- Ask the children to TTYP to explain to each other what *flashback* means. Collect feedback and clarify where necessary.
- Tell the children that writers can use flashback to create powerful links between present and past events and characters in a story.
- Explain that when Lou Kuenzler wrote *Gone Away!* she used flashback to tell us more about the friendship between Brendan and the narrator, Leon, and to reveal the truth about their relationship.
- Display the **CD (file 4.2)** to show examples of shifts in the narrative between the past and the present in *Gone Away!* Ask the children to TTYP to try to identify the point in each text where the shift occurs. Take feedback.
- Click on the 'Highlights' icon to highlight the present and past parts of each sample of text.
- Now ask the children to TTYP to discuss what the flashbacks tell us about the changing feelings Leon has about his friendship with Brendan.
- Take feedback and give your own opinion, supporting your ideas with examples from the text.

noting ideas

Daily log

Purpose: for children to keep a personal reading, writing and thinking log in order to record thoughts and ideas for their own writing

- Ask the children to TTYP to discuss what advice they would give to Leon to help him to cope with the loss of Brendan.
- Tell them to write a couple of their suggestions in their Daily log.

Fiction: Stories with flashbacks

Curriculum link: effective discussion; provide justifications for their views

Big Question ⓒⅅ

Purpose: for children to develop their skills of argument and discussion through a mini enquiry session based on a philosophical question relating to the work of the day

- Display today's Big Question on the **CD (file 4.3)**:

  If the past exists, where is it?

- Follow the process explained at the end of Day 1 (p.91).

DAY 5

drawing inferences and justifying with evidence, identifying key details that support ideas

What if not...?

Purpose: for children to consider how chronology, narration and character each affects the other

- Ask the children to look at the What if not...? questions in the Pupils' Book p.37. Model how you consider the first What if not...? What if not *Leon* narrating? What if *Brendan narrated the flashbacks?*
- TOL: I think we would get a very different view of their friendship. I suppose Brendan could make Leon sound really weak, after all, he seemed to be able to boss his friend about and he might have bragged about being able to make him do his homework for him. On the other hand, perhaps Brendan didn't realise how mean he was to his friend Leon sometimes. If he thought he was just being amusing, he might have made the story about the sleepover sound like great fun for Leon rather than humiliating and hurtful.
- Ask children to TTYP and discuss this and the other What if not...? questions. Collect feedback and encourage others to build upon the argument. Give your opinion too.

Dramatic reconstruction ⓒⅅ

Purpose: for children to become familiar with a scenario that could be used later for writing

- Remind the children that one of the What if not...? questions explored how things would be different in the story if Brendan had not died but had simply moved away. Explain that they are going to create a role-play based on this idea.
- Tell the children that in their scene, Leon has gone to visit Brendan at his new home. He hasn't seen him for a long time and he has been thinking about what Sam said about Brendan treating him like dirt. Tell them to read that section of the text in the Anthology p.49.
- Ask the children to TTYP to discuss what might happen or be said in these circumstances.
- Give one copy of printable **CD (file 5.1)** to each set of partners. Ask them to use it to plan their role-play.
- As the children perform their role-plays, walk around noting points to mention in your feedback, e.g. empathetic responses and imaginative interaction between characters.

noting ideas, provide reasoned justifications for their views

Daily log

Purpose: for children to keep a personal reading, writing and thinking log in order to record thoughts and ideas for their own writing

- Ask the children to TTYP to discuss which character in the story *Gone Away!* they felt most empathy with, or sympathy for, and why. Tell them to record their opinions in their Daily log.

Curriculum link:
effective discussion; provide justifications for their views

Big Question (CD)

Purpose: for children to develop their skills of argument and discussion through a mini enquiry session based on a philosophical question relating to the work of the day

- Display today's Big Question on the **CD (file 5.2)**:

  Should best friends always tell each other the truth?

- Follow the process explained at the end of Day 1 (p.91).

WRITING FICTION

DAY 6

understand, through being shown, the skills and processes essential for writing

Build a beginning A (CD) PB

Purpose: for children to be able to write an effective opening of a story that engages the reader straight away

- Tell the children that you want to create a great opening for a story you are thinking of writing. You need to make sure the reader is interested from the start and wants to read on to find out what happens next.
- Say that you have chosen to base your story around two of your favourite Word power words from *Gone Away!* – *nonchalant* and *vengeful*.
- Point to the words on your word wall and remind the children of where they were used in *Gone Away!* in the Anthology (pages 40 and 41). Repeat the definitions and sentences from Day 3: *nonchalant* – casual, cool, laid-back
  He tried hard to look *nonchalant* when he went out with his new hair cut for the first time!
  vengeful – wanting revenge, unforgiving
  The victim was *vengeful* and full of bitterness.
- Tell the children that the phrase 'giant, vengeful jelly' in the text gave you an idea for a story about a boy who runs out of hair gel and uses jelly instead.
- Display the **CD (file 6.1)** to show 'your' first draft of a beginning using those words. Read it out loud to the class.
- Explain that this was your first attempt and you were not happy with it. It was too dull. Click on the 'Prompts' icon and ask the children to TTYP to use the prompts to evaluate it as the beginning of a story.
- Collect feedback and encourage lots of critical discussion. It is important that you keep referring back to the text on the screen, pointing to relevant sections as children make their comments.
- Now display the **CD (file 6.2)** to show the re-worked beginning. Explain that the black text is from the first draft and the highlighted text shows additions and alterations in syntax, punctuation and sentence length.
- Navigate to the second screen to display the prompts and ask the children to TTYP to use the prompts to evaluate it as the beginning of a story.
- Collect feedback and encourage lots of critical discussion. Again, refer back to the text on the screen, pointing to relevant sections as children make their comments.
- Now tell the children to look at the dull paragraph in the Pupils' Book p.38 which was written from the wasp's point of view.
- Ask them to TTYP to discuss ways of making it more engaging for the reader and to add a sentence designed to make the reader want to know what happens next.
- When the children are happy with their opening sentence, they can begin writing. Decide whether you want the children to continue to work with their partners or on their own.

Tell a story

Purpose: for children to develop confidence in building a story orally

- Tell the children that they are going read the hair jelly story from the beginning again and then move the story on *orally* with their partners. Model the process first. Display the beginning on **CD (file 6.2)** again, read it out loud and then make up the next sentence or two. Don't make it look too easy. Hesitate, change your mind about a word or idea, but don't take too long!
- Explain to the children that they will swap roles from teller to listener and vice versa when you say "swap and stop" at about 30 second intervals (two or three times), continuing the story from that point each time. Emphasis should be on building confidence in storytelling and keeping the audience engaged.
- Walk around listening in and noting points to share in your feedback.

Curriculum link: noting ideas

Daily log

Purpose: for children to keep a personal reading, writing and thinking log in order to record thoughts and ideas for their own writing

- Ask the children to write down one of the ideas they or their partner came up with for continuing the story.

effective discussion; provide justifications for their views

Big Question

Purpose: for children to develop their skills of argument and discussion through a mini enquiry session based on a philosophical question relating to the work of the day

- Display today's Big Question on the **CD (file 6.3)**:

  Which is more important in life – beginnings or endings?

- Follow the process as explained at the end of Day 1 (p.91).

DAY 7

Build a story 1

Purpose: for children to be able to see a story grow through three stages of development

understand, through being shown, the skills and processes essential for writing

- Remind the children that they heard two versions of *Gone Away!* (Story versions 1 & 2) before they heard and read the full story. It prepared them to read the full story.
- Explain that you are going to show them two versions of a new story to be written based on the idea of the boy and his hair gel. These versions prepared the writer to write the full story. Show questions on the **CD (file 7.1)** and explain that these were the prompts that helped the writer to know what to put in the new story. Take the role of writer for these activites.
- Now display Build a story 1 on the **CD (file 7.2)**.
- Read the points out loud to the children. Explain that you are now going to show them another version of the new story to be written. This one has additional information and words – it has been developed.

making comparisons

Build a story 2

Purpose: for children to be able to see a story grow through three stages of development

- Show Build a story 2 on the **CD (file 7.3)** and read it out loud to the children.
- Then Click 'Highlights' to show additional information, synonyms and adjectives. TOL as you compare this version with Build a story 1. Synonyms that appear within Build a story 2 have been highlighted. Ask children if they can also identify any synonyms that have been used to replace words that appeared in Build a story 1.

Build a story 3

> *Curriculum link:*
> *using similar writing as models for their own*

Purpose: for children to see an example of writing that will provide a model for their own writing

- An example story is provided as a model for writing. Remain in the role of the writer of this story during these activities. Display the story on the **CD (file 7.4)**. Explain that when writing this story, your purpose was to entertain and interest the audience or reader.
- Read 'your' story (Build a story 3) from the **CD (file 7.4)** to the children.

Evaluation

> *assessing the effectiveness of others' writing*

Purpose: for children to develop their ability to evaluate the effectiveness of a piece of writing

- Print out copies of the story for the children from the **CD (file 7.5)**. Ask them to TTYP to read alternate paragraphs of the story.
- Using TTYP and oral feedback, ask the children to evaluate the writing using the Build a story 3 guide questions in the Pupils' Book p.39. Collect feedback and encourage discussion and constructive criticism.

Daily log

> *noting ideas, provide reasoned justifications for their views*

Purpose: for children to keep a personal reading, writing and thinking log in order to record thoughts and ideas for their own writing

- Ask the children to share ideas for a title for the story. Ask them to record their best idea in their Daily log and explain why they think it is a good title.

Big Question

> *effective discussion, provide justifications for their views*

Purpose: for children to develop their skills of argument and discussion through a mini enquiry session based on a philosophical question relating to the work of the day

- Display today's Big Question on the **CD (file 7.6)**:

  Does a person's appearance tell us what kind of person they are?

- Follow the process as explained at the end of Day 1 (p.91).

Write a story 1

> *using similar writing as models for their own*

Purpose: for children to become familiar with phrases that signal movement in time

- Tell the children that you would like the hair gel and the wasp story to include flashbacks like the story *Gone Away!*
- Explain that you have collected some phrases called 'signals of time' to let the reader know that the narrative is moving backwards or forwards in time.
- Display the **CD (file 8.1)** to show examples of signals of time.
- Read them out loud and use MT/YT to help the children to become familiar with the phrases.

Write a story 2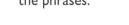

> *using devices to build cohesion*

Purpose: for children to understand how depth and interest can be created in a narrative by including flashback

- Display the **CD (file 8.2)** to show the numbered story board squares for the basic wasp story.
- Click on the 'TOL' icon to show the think bubbles. Use these to TOL about how you could use time signals to include flashback in the story.
- Display **CD (file 8.3)** to show your new opening using flashback. Use the think bubbles to explain the process.

- Now display **CD (file 8.4)** and ask the children to TTYP to discuss the questions in the speech call-out. Collect feedback and clarify points where necessary.

Curriculum link: noting ideas

Daily log

Purpose: for children to keep a personal reading, writing and thinking log in order to record thoughts and ideas for their own writing

- Tell the children to TTYP to discuss what the conversation might be between the coolest girl in the school and her best friend after Danny's humiliating exit. Tell them to do a very short improvisation and then record the conversation in their Daily log.

effective discussion; provide justifications for their views

Big Question

Purpose: for children to develop their skills of argument and discussion through a mini enquiry session based on a philosophical question relating to the work of the day

- Display today's Big Question on the **CD (file 8.5)**:

  Is it true that if you never make a mistake, you will never achieve anything?

- Follow the process as explained at the end of Day I (p.91).

DAY 9

Write a story 3

Purpose: for children to use a storyboard and signals of time to write their own story with flashbacks

describing settings, characters and atmosphere, using devices to build cohesion within and across paragraphs

- Tell the children that they are now ready to plan their own story based on part of *Gone Away!* Remind them about the grid they filled in on Day 5 about a meeting between Brendan and Leon, based on the idea that Brendan hadn't died, just moved away. Display **CD (file 9.1)** to show the grid again. Ask children to feed back some of the ideas they put into their grids and scribe them onto your grid.
- Explain that they are going to develop this idea into a short story with flashbacks.
- Give each child a printout from the **CD (file 9.2)** and some scissors. Now tell them to cut out the storyboard squares and the selection of signals of time.
- Explain that you want them to move the squares around to help them to plan the sequence of their story and to experiment with the time signal squares to move the story backwards and forwards.
- Display **CD (file 9.3)** to model the process. TOL about the effect of the different sequences and the use of flashback. Stress the importance of experimenting and evaluating the effectiveness of their ideas rather than finishing the activity quickly.
- When they are happy with their plan, ask them to use the guidance in the Write a story 3 activity in the Pupils' Book p.39 to flesh out each square/section of their story. Point out that they should be careful to punctuate any dialogue correctly. Remind them to make use of any parts of their Daily log and the Anthology to help them to carry out the task. Explain that the storyboard squares were intended to be used as a guide for their planning and they may find they want to move the information within the squares to different places in the story.
- Encourage children to discuss their ideas with their partners before they begin to write.

DAY 10

Share a story

Purpose: for children to be able to look critically at their writing

assessing the effectiveness of their own and others' writing

- Ask the children to read through their own stories, underlining their favourite parts. Ask them to share these with their partners. Collect feedback on favourite bits from partners.
- Make sure that any powerful or rarer words or phrases used are added to the word wall.

Evaluate and edit (CD)

Purpose: for children to evaluate their own and their partner's work against specific criteria and then discuss how they could improve their work

- Display **CD (file 10.1)** to show the evaluation prompts and read them together using MT/YT.
- As a model, select an example of work from the children where the writing has met the criteria, and share this with the other children, explaining why it works well.
- Tell the children to take turns to read their partner's writing and discuss how well they have met the criteria.
- Ask children to discuss at least two changes they could make to improve their work following the partner discussion.

Curriculum link: proofread for spelling and punctuation errors

Proofread

Purpose: for children to proofread their work and make changes to improve the accuracy of their grammar, punctuation and spelling

- Now ask the children to proofread their work. If you have noticed that several children need to improve on a particular aspect of spelling, grammar or punctuation, use this as a focus for the Proofread activity. Write an example which includes common errors from the children's writing and use this as a model.
- The children should always be checking for standard use of punctuation and correct spelling of common exception words.
- The following points would be relevant as the particular focus for this Unit:
  - check for consistent use of the first person and past tense
  - check that speech is punctuated correctly.

effective discussion; provide justifications for their views, distinguish between fact and opinion

Very Big Question

Purpose: for children to explore one of the Big Questions in more depth

- See Unit 1 Day 10 for teaching notes on the Very Big Question p.36.

Biography and autobiography

READING AND WRITING NON-FICTION

In the non-fiction part of the Unit biographical and autobiographical reading and writing will be explored. Children will use a variety of resources to research a biographical subject. They will create a PowerPoint presentation of a biography and go on to write their own autobiographies.

See p.88 for the daily timetable for the Non-fiction week.

Non-fiction

Reading

Children will:

- explore different types of biographical material such as birth certificates, reports and diaries
- identify the key features of biographical writing
- decide what they want to know about Daniel Radcliffe before they read his biography, to focus their reading.

Writing

Key writing purpose to be shared with the children:

To write a biography about the life of Alexander Selkirk and present it to the class.

Writing evaluation to be shared with the children

My biography:

- includes information about the key people and events in Alexander Selkirk's life, to inform and entertain the reader
- includes dates and/or a timeline
- is organised in a way that is engaging and easy to understand.

Grammar:

- uses third person and past tense throughout the biography
- uses adverbials of time to structure information.

See the Planning section of the Software ('Timetables' tab) for a printable version of the Writing purpose and evaluation.

DAY 11

Curriculum link:
learn the
conventions of
different types
of writing

Introduction

Purpose: for children to be able to link one of the Big Questions and the fiction text studied in weeks 1 and 2 with non-fiction biographical and autobiographical writing

- Show the Big Question from Day 1 on the **CD (file 1.4)**:

  Can we ever really know what living in the past was like?

- Ask the children to TTYP to recall some of the thoughts and ideas they had in their discussion. Collect feedback.

- Remind the children that they now know that writers of fiction often use *flashback* as a way of revisiting and recreating people, times and places that have gone forever – the writer can transport a character and a reader to the past and back to the present again.

- Explain that the non-fiction text types *biography* and *autobiography* also use flashback as a way of recreating the past to tell us about a person's life. Tell the children that this is the type of non-fiction writing that they are going to look at this week.

- Display the **CD (file 11.1)** to show the definitions of biographical and autobiographical through the prefixes and root word – *auto, bio* and *graphical*. Write these definitions on cards and start a *biography* and *autobiography* word wall.

- Ask the children to make a note of, and pass on to you, any other words they come across at school or at home that have the prefix *auto*.

Biographical writing

Purpose: for children to become familiar with different types of biographical writing

- Tell the children that any writing that is about another person's life can be called biographical writing.

- Explain that a writer who is writing a biography about someone will need to find and read as much information about that person as possible. Ask them to TTYP to think of what a writer could use to help them to find out about a person, e.g. *letters, birth certificates, school reports, interviews*.

- Collect feedback and write some key examples they give on cards to display on your word wall.

- Display the **CD (file 11.2)** to show some examples of biographical information. Explain that a writer has started to collect these examples to help them to research and write about someone who was once one of the most famous people in the world. Read through the texts.

- Navigate through the screens to display the Biography research grid. Click 'TOL' and use the speech bubbles to help you to show how the writer has located key information from the texts and recorded it in the grid.

asking questions
to improve their
understanding,
retrieve information

Your research

Purpose: for children to be able to use a variety of resources to research a biographical subject

- Explain to the children that they are going to find out about another famous person, the Harry Potter film actor, Daniel Radcliffe.

- Give each set of partners a copy of the Biography research grid printed out from the **CD (file 11.3)**.

- Ask the children to TTYP to make a list of research questions to use to find the answers about Daniel Radcliffe and to add these questions to the research grid.

- Tell them to use the Internet and/or the school library to find out more about the actor Daniel Radcliffe and fill out the rest of the grid.

- Remind the children that various websites on the Internet could be used to find information such as websites with reviews of Daniel's acting and those which have interviews with the actor. The children could look on sites such as Daniel's own official website, the BBC's *Newsround* website or the Harry Potter films website.
- Tell the children to complete for homework if necessary and collect it in the next day.

Curriculum link:
noting ideas

Daily log

Purpose: for children to keep a personal reading, writing and thinking log in order to record thoughts and ideas for their own writing

- Remind the children that *auto* means *self* and so an *autobiography* is a text someone has written about their own life.
- Tell the children to record at least four important or memorable events in their own lives, e.g. moving house, the birth of a sibling, starting school, a special treat, getting chicken pox, going on holiday, learning to ride a bike, staying away from home for the first time, and then put them in chronological order giving dates, or approximate dates, where possible.
- Ask them to decide which event is the most significant one and why and ask them to record their thoughts in their Daily log.

DAY 12

making comparisons

Think and link

Purpose: for children to be able to make connections between fiction and non-fiction texts

- Display the **CD (file 12.1)** to remind the children of the classic fiction story *Robinson Crusoe* which they looked at in Week 1. Explain that the writer Daniel Defoe based his fictional story on real events that happened to a man called Alexander Selkirk who lived more than three hundred years ago.
- Explain that we have lots of information about the man often called the real Robinson Crusoe, Alexander Selkirk, from old documents, websites and different biographies that have been written about him.
- Tell the children that these non-fiction biographical texts can help us to find out about some key events in Selkirk's amazing life.

exploring the meaning of words in context

Word power

Purpose: for children to develop their knowledge of and application of rarer vocabulary taken from the text and for children to understand how writers use language for effect

> plunder   disintegrated   unfortunate   vociferous   disharmony

- Tell the children that some of the texts about Alexander Selkirk have lots of words and phrases that are not commonly used in our everyday conversations.
- Display the words and phrases on the **CD (file 12.2)**. Look at them with the children and read the sentences to them. Ask them to repeat the sentences using MT/YT, giving dramatic emphasis and actions as you all say them.
- Print out the words and definitions from the **CD (file 12.3)** and display on your Power words wall.
- Now tell the children to do the Word power activity in the Pupils' Book p.40.
- Find opportunities to use the words yourself during the day, e.g. 'No matter how *vociferous* you are, I won't change my mind!' Encourage them to use the words at home with friends and family so that they become embedded in the children's own spoken (and eventually, written) vocabulary.

- Do a quick vocabulary check for any other words or phrases you think might need clarifying, e.g. *privateer, commended to the deep.*

Deconstruction 1 🅐

Curriculum link: using similar writing as models for their own

Purpose: for children to see examples of writing that will provide models for their own writing

- Ask the children to look at the biographical information about Alexander Selkirk in the Anthology pp.51–53. TOL about the key features that help you to identify the different text types of diary/log book entry, biography, birth certificate and website.
- Remind the children to check the word wall or their Pupils' Books for tricky words and phrases.
- Now tell the children to TTYP to read through the Selkirk texts, taking turns to read a few sentences each.
- Ask them to TTYP to decide what the key events were in Selkirk's life. Collect feedback and scribe on the board. Ask the children to help you to number the events to show their chronology.

Daily log

exploring the meaning of words in context

Purpose: for children to keep a personal reading, writing and thinking log in order to record thoughts and ideas for their own writing

- Ask the children to choose up to five Power words to describe Alexander Selkirk at different times in his life, e.g. *brave, foolish, adventurous, selfish.*
- Ask them to find synonyms for at least two of their words.
- Tell them to record the words and synonyms in their Daily log.
- Collect feedback and write some of their words on cards to add to your word wall.

DAY 13

Write a biography 1 🆑 🅐

retrieve, record and present information from non-fiction

Purpose: for children to develop their ability to select and retrieve key information and present it in a different form

- Display the **CD (file 13.1)** to show a timeline. Tell the children that you made this timeline based on the information they found out about Daniel Radcliffe.
- Explain that this is a simple, linear representation of significant events in Daniel Radcliffe's life. Remind the children that they retrieved or collected lots of biographical information from different sources and that you have presented it in a different, simple form.
- Tell the children they are going to create a timeline of key events in Alexander Selkirk's life. Ask them to TTYP to recall the key events they identified yesterday. Remind them to go back to the original sources in the Anthology pp.51–53 if they need to.
- They can draw the timeline in their Daily log to use as a source for their Selkirk biographies.

Deconstruction 2 🆑 🅐

learn the conventions of different types of writing

Purpose: for children to develop their understanding of the key features of biographical writing

- Tell the children to find the texts about Alexander Selkirk in the Anthology pp.51–53.
- Explain that they are now going to use these texts to create a biography of Alexander Selkirk as a PowerPoint presentation and that their audience will be their peers.
- Display the **CD (file 13.2)** to show the key features of a good biography and talk through each slide, relating points to the Anthology texts and work completed in previous lessons.

Non-fiction: Biography and autobiography

Curriculum link:
plan their writing

Write a biography 2 PB A

Purpose: for children to be able to create a biography in electronic form for a specific audience

- Ask the children to use all the tips in the Pupils' Book p.41 to help them to plan their PowerPoint biographies of Alexander Selkirk. You may wish to show them the **CD (file 13.2)** again.
- Tell them to draft each slide on paper. Ask them to note what information they want to include, the sources they already have, the further research they have to do and the sources of the further research.
- Now tell the children to begin creating their PowerPoint biographies as soon as they are ready.
- Remind the children to look in their Daily log at the words and synonyms they used to describe Alexander Selkirk. Tell them to try to use some of these words and/or synonyms in their biographies of Selkirk.

summarising
the main ideas,
identifying key
details that support
the main ideas

Daily log

Purpose: for children to keep a personal reading, writing and thinking log in order to record thoughts and ideas for their own writing

- Tell the children they are going to be creating a detailed mind map of their own lives over the next two days in preparation for writing their autobiographies at the end of the week.
- Model how you might start a mind map of your own life. TOL as you choose which headings you want for your 'branches', e.g. *family, appearance, interests, school and work, homes,* or simply *past, present, future* with lots of sub-headings/branches.
- Now tell them to record in their Daily log, at least three questions to ask their parents or carers about their birth and very early childhood.
- Ask them to begin to create their mind maps based on what they already know about themselves and their lives.
- Remind them to ask the questions they have thought of so that they can develop their mind maps tomorrow.

DAY 14

Write a biography 3

Purpose: for children to complete, edit and refine their biographies

developing ideas

- Tell the children that they have most of this lesson to complete their Selkirk PowerPoint biographies. Explain that tomorrow they are going to show these to their partners and evaluate each other's biographies.
- Allow time for the children to complete their PowerPoints.

proofread for
spelling and
punctuation errors

Proofread

Purpose: for children to proofread their work and make changes to improve the accuracy of their grammar, punctuation and spelling

- Now ask the children to proofread their work. If you have noticed that several children need to improve on a particular aspect of spelling, grammar or punctuation, use this as a focus for the Proofread activity. Write an example which includes common errors from the children's writing and use this as a model.
- The children should always be checking for standard use of punctuation and correct spelling of common exception words.
- The following points would be relevant as the particular focus for this Unit:
  - check that the third person and past tense is used consistently
  - check that *Alexander Selkirk* is spelled correctly
  - check that capital letters are used for proper nouns.

Curriculum link:
present information
from non-fiction

Daily log

*Purpose: for children to keep a personal reading, writing and thinking log in order to record
thoughts and ideas for their own writing*

- Ask the children to TTYP to share some of the answers they collected from
parents and carers based on the questions they asked for homework.
- Tell the children to continue to work on the mind map of their own life adding in
new information.
- Explain that good biographers and autobiographers look at what historical events
were happening in the world at the same time as private events were taking place
in people's lives, e.g. the moon landing, royal weddings, wars beginning or ending.
Ask them to try to find out what historical or significant public events were
happening in the year that they were born.
- Tell them to keep recording further questions or points to research as they think
of them.

Biography presentations

Purpose: for children to show their presentations to their partners

- Tell the children they are now going to show their PowerPoint presentations to
their partners. Explain that Partner 1s will show their presentations to Partner 2s
first and then they will swap roles.

perform their own
compositions

Evaluate and edit

assessing the
effectiveness of
their own and
others' writing

*Purpose: for children to evaluate their own and their partner's work against specific criteria
and then discuss how they could improve their work*

- Display **CD (file 15.1)** to show the evaluation prompts and read them together
using MT/YT.
- As a model, select an example of a presentation where the children met the
criteria, and share with the other children why it worked well.
- Tell the children to discuss with their partner how well they met the criteria.
- Ask children to discuss at least two changes they could make to improve their
presentation following the partner discussion.

developing ideas,
drawing on
research

Write an autobiography

*Purpose: for children to compose an autobiographical account, based on their research and
mind maps*

- Tell the children that for homework, they are going to write two paragraphs of
their autobiographies based on a key event in their lives.
- Remind them that they have already listed some key events in their Daily log,
created a mind map of their lives and conducted research with parents and carers.
- Tell the children to use these resources and to look at the examples from two
autobiographies and the questions in the Pupils' Book p.42 to help them.
- Ask them to read through the two examples and then TTYP to discuss the
questions.
- Collect feedback and encourage the children to think about the style of the
opening of their own autobiography.
- Give each pupil a copy of the autobiography guide printed out from the
CD (file 15.2) to take home to help them to compose their autobiographical
paragraphs.
N.B. You may wish to allow more time for the children to develop their
autobiographies further and present them in booklet form.

Fiction: Narrative and plays
Non-fiction: Persuasive texts

Timetable

WEEK 1   Reading fiction   *The Elephant in the Room*

Day 1	Day 2	Day 3	Day 4	Day 5
The script store	Word power 1 📄	Word power 2 📄	Re-read a script version 3	Role on the wall 📄
Conventions of form	Read a script version 3	Grammar: hyphens to avoid confusion	What's explicit, what's implicit?	Drama
Read a script version 1	Clarify	Re read a script version 3	Dramatic improvisation 📄	Daily log
Read a script version 2	Think and link	What if not...?	Daily log	Big Question
Daily log	Daily log	Daily log	Big Question	
Big Question	Big Question	Big Question		

WEEK 2   Writing fiction   *The Elephant in the Room*

Day 6	Day 7	Day 8	Day 9	Day 10
Build a character	Dramatic improvisation	Evaluation 📄	Write a script 3	Share a script
Show, don't tell	Build a script 1	Write a script 1 📄		Evaluate and edit
Build a speech	Build a script 2	Write a script 2		Proofread
Daily log	Build a script 3	Daily log		Very Big Question
Big Question	Daily log	Big Question		
	Big Question			

WEEK 3   Reading and writing non–fiction   Persuasive texts

Day 11	Day 12	Day 13	Day 14	Day 15
Introduction	Deconstruction 1	Deconstruction 2	Deconstruction 3 📄	Persuasive presentations
Word power 📄	Read a persuasive text 📄	Role-play	Write to persuade	Daily log
Bias		Improve a persuasive text	Proofread	Evaluate and edit
Fact vs opinion				
Daily log				

📄: shows that a file should be printed out from the Software.

Overview of the Unit

In the fiction part of this Unit children study a playscript, *The Elephant in the Room,* about a child-carer. The author, Lou Kuenzler, uses dramatic conventions, such as monologue, to involve the audience and create atmosphere whilst exploring the difficult subject of parental mental health issues in a sensitive and provoking way. Children study the plot, characters and dramatic conventions. Elements of performance are also included. They build a character and explore the stages of development of a script, then go on to write an extra scene for the play.

In the linked non-fiction part of the Unit persuasive texts are studied, looking at biased articles, advertorials and adverts. Children write a scripted presentation and use it to persuade the class to vote either for or against the use of a brain boosting memory aid in schools. For more information about the Non-fiction week and the Non-fiction writing evaluation criteria, see p.124.

The Homework Book provides a homework activity related to the content of this Unit for each of the three weeks.

Playscripts

Reading

Children will:

- understand how a monologue reveals the inner thoughts of a character to the audience
- explore characters' thoughts using implicit and explicit information given in the play
- explore the characters' thoughts and feelings further, through dramatic reconstruction.

Writing

Key writing purpose to be shared with the children:

To write a new scene for the play, including a monologue for a new character I have created.

Writing evaluation to be shared with the children

My scene:

- builds a new character to represent the emotion of guilt
- includes a build-up and a resolution that develops a story and sustains tension
- includes speech and thoughts which are appropriate for the characters.

Grammar:

- uses adjectives to give depth and detail to the playscript.

See the Planning section of the Software ('Timetables' tab) for a printable version of the Writing purpose and evaluation.

Fiction: Narrative and plays
The Elephant in the Room by Lou Kuenzler

READING FICTION

Resources

PB Pupils' Book, pp.43–51

A Anthology, pp.54–67

CD CD on interactive whiteboard (Unit 5)

GB Grammar Bank on CD

HB Homework Book, pp.17–19

DAY 1

Curriculum link:
learn the conventions of different types of writing

The script store (CD)

Purpose: for children to understand what a monologue is and how they can be used in playscripts

- Display the two play extracts on the **CD (file 1.1)**.
- Tell the children that when one character speaks on their own for a long time in a play it is called a *monologue*. Explain that mono is a prefix that means one *and* -logue means *speech*.
- Focus on the Dame Dotty speech and read it for comic effect. Ask the children to TTYP and discuss what type of play might have a comic dame in it.
- Ask the children to TTYP and choose two lines from the first screen that they like and say them to each other in role as the dame.
- Ask the children to TTYP and discuss what they think of the dame. Do they find him funny? Can they find any examples of word play in the speech? (e.g. *dotty*) Can anyone think of why he might talk to the audience like this? (*For comic effect, to engage them in the play, to set up the action and suspense i.e. 'have you seen anyone suspicious?'*)
- Display the *Alice in Wonderland* speech and read it. Ask the children to TTYP and discuss whether it is a monologue. Is there any part of it that it not a monologue?
- Direct the children to the stage directions and ask them to TTYP and read one part of the monologue to each other using the stage directions to help them.
- Ask the children to TTYP and discuss how the monologue helped them to get to know the character.

Conventions of form (CD)

Purpose: for children to revise the conventions of the form of a playscript

- Remind the children that there are rules about the layout of scripts so that everyone involved in the play knows exactly what to say and what to do.
- Click on the **CD (file 1.2)**. Use the speech bubbles to explain the basic features and conventions of scripts.
- Explain that in a full script there would also be a list of the characters, called the cast.
- Tell the children they are now going to hear the bare bones of a full playscript and we are going to call it Script version 1.

read plays

Read a script version 1 (CD)

Purpose: for children to become familiar with Script version 1, the bare bones of the The Elephant in the Room

- Read Script version 1 aloud all the way through to the children. (Do not reveal any surprises or the ending of the final play.)

  Script version 1

  Characters

  - **Girl 1**   – **Girl 2**
  - **Girl 1's dad**   – **Elephant**

Scene 1

Friday afternoon

Action

1. The girls are waiting for a bus.
2. They are late.
3. They talk about plans for the weekend and a party.
4. Girl 1 is worried.

Scene 2

Girl 1's home

Action

1. Girl 1's dad is upset.
2. Girl 1 tells her dad about the party.
3. Her dad says she cannot go.
4. Girl 1 says she has too much homework anyway.
5. The dad tries to make her feel better.

Scene 3

Monday morning

Action

1. The two girls meet again at the bus stop and talk about their weekends.

- Use My turn/Your turn (MT/YT) and TTYP for each point. Use exaggerated intonation and emphasis where appropriate. This is to help the children to hold the basic script in their heads.
- Display Script version 1 on the **CD (file 1.3)** for the children to read.

Curriculum link: identifying how language, structure, and presentation contribute to meaning

Read a script version 2 (CD)

Purpose: for children to examine how Script version 2 provides additional information for the reader and for children to become more familiar with the script before they hear the full version

- Tell the children that they are now going to hear a fuller version of the script. Explain that it will tell them more about the characters and the action.
- Read Script version 2 out loud with appropriate enthusiasm and intonation.

Script version 2

Characters

- **Lina**   – **Caitlin**
- **Mr Chang (Lina's dad)**   – **Elephant**

Scene 1

Late Friday afternoon at the bus stop, Caitlin is holding a small carrier bag.

Action

1. Lina and Caitlin are waiting for a bus, after a shopping trip in town.
2. They are late and Lina is anxious.
3. They talk about plans for the weekend, i.e. the insect life project and Tanya's birthday disco.
4. Lina is worried about being late and Caitlin teases her by saying that she bets that Lina will do nothing except stay in and colour in work for her project all weekend.

Scene 2

Lina's home, which is a small flat

Action

1. Lina's dad, Mr Chang, is upset and looks dishevelled.
2. Lina tells her dad about the party, which makes him even more distraught.
3. Her dad says she cannot go. He gets more agitated as he worries that no one will look after him if she is gone.
4. Lina shrugs and says she has too much homework anyway.
5. Her dad tries to make her feel better by telling her about the amazing adventures that they will have when he gets better.

Scene 3

Fade up to Monday morning

Action

1. The two girls meet again at the bus stop and talk about their weekends.

- Now display this version on the **CD (file 1.4)**. Click on the highlighter tool to identify the additional information:
    - We now know characters' names – *Lina, Caitlin, Mr Chang*.
    - Addition of the information that *Lina is worried about being late*.
    - Addition of the fact that the relationship between the two girls is not equal – *Caitlin teases Lina*.
    - We now know that the dad is easily upset and agitated and can infer that he might be unwell.
    - We now know more about the setting, 'a small flat,' and the stage directions.
    - Additional information that Lina's dad tries to make her feel better by talking about the future, when he hopes he will be better.
- TOL and use TTYP to share how this extra information changes the pictures in our minds, our thoughts and ideas about the characters and events as we hear the script.
- Notice that the elephant is mentioned in the cast but not in the script yet. Ask the children to TTYP and discuss what it could be.

Curriculum link:
noting initial ideas

Daily log

Purpose: for children to keep a personal reading, writing and thinking log in order to record thoughts and ideas for their own writing

- See the notes in Unit 1 (p.24).
- Explain to the children that they are going to continue to collect thoughts and ideas in their Daily log.
- Ask the children to TTYP to discuss what Lina and Caitlin talk about when they meet up on Monday morning. Ask them to record one or two ideas about how the conversation might go.

effective discussion; provide justifications for their views

Big Question (CD)

Purpose: for children to develop their skills of argument and discussion through a mini enquiry session based on a philosophical question relating to the work of the day

- Display today's Big Question on the **CD (file 1.5)**.

    Are all friendships fair?

- Ask the children to TTYP to discuss. Collect feedback from partners and scribe some responses. Tell the children that each day's Big Question and their thoughts will be collected on the CD and saved so that at the end of Week 2 they can then vote on which question to discuss more deeply. See Introduction for further notes (p.13).

DAY 2

Curriculum link:
exploring the meaning of words in context

Word power 1

Purpose: for children to increase their knowledge and application of synonyms and to examine how writers use language for effect

> worried   anxious   nervous   apprehensive   uneasy   concerned   tense
> upset   agitated   distraught   troubled   frantic   distressed

- Tell the children that there are some words in Script version 2 that mean the same as *upset* in Script version 1. Tell them that these *synonyms* can show different ways of being upset (*distraught* and *agitated*).
- Display Script version 2 on the **CD (file 2.1)** and then click 'Synonyms' to identify the synonyms for *worried*.
- Repeat the procedure on the second screen to identify the synonyms for *upset*.
- Display synonyms for *worried* on the **CD (file 2.2)** and TOL, explaining what the words mean. Ask the children to TTYP to discuss how intense each word is. Take feedback and then drag and drop each of the synonyms onto the target, placing the most intense word in the Bull's eye, the least intense word on the outside and the others in between. TOL about your decisions.
- Navigate to the next screen and repeat the procedure with synonyms for *upset*. Note that some of the synonyms will be similar to both worried and upset. They have been separated for the purposes of this activity to emphasise the emotions in each of the scenes.
- Print all of these words and phrases using the **CD (file 2.3)** and display them on your word wall.
- TOL and use TTYP to share an example of how these words change the pictures in our heads as we hear the scripts.

explain and discuss their understanding of what they have read

Read a script version 3 PB

Purpose: for children to hear and enjoy the full version of the script for the first time

- Tell the children they are now going to hear the whole script for the first time. Show your enthusiasm before you start. TOL about which parts you can't wait to hear about, etc.
- Display the **CD (file 2.4)** and play the audio to hear the playscript read by actors.
- At the end of the story, ask the children to TTYP to discuss the Script version 3 questions in their Pupils' Books p.43. Then collect feedback.
- Make links to the notes the children made in their Daily log about what Lina and Caitlin would talk about whilst waiting for a bus on Monday. Ask the children to TTYP and discuss whether they think Lina is telling the truth.

consider how authors have developed characters

Clarify

Purpose: for children to link the dramatic effects to their understanding of the play

- Go through the play using the TOL on the **CD (file 2.5)** to identify some obvious examples of how the playwright creates atmosphere, gives direction and tells us about the characters.
- Ask the children to TTYP and discuss how the elephant interacts with the audience.

Curriculum link:
summarising the
main ideas

Think and link (CD)

Purpose: for children to understand the chronology and main points of the play

- Reveal the playscript map on the **CD (file 2.6)** and go through it using TOL to discuss what the main events are. Draw the children's attention to the point where the elephant shrinks and Mr Chang is able to comfort his daughter.
- Ask the children to TTYP to discuss what they think Lina is thinking as she talks to her friend at the bus stop. Take feedback and scribe onto the thought bubble.

summarising
the main ideas,
identifying key
details

Daily log (CD)

Purpose: for children to create a written or drawn representation of the story that can be used as an aide memoire

- Ask the children to map the play themselves – you may wish to display the CD version to support them, **CD (file 2.6)**. Encourage them to add details especially of how the elephant controls the atmosphere of the play.

effective
discussion; provide
justifications for
their views

Big Question

Purpose: for children to develop their skills of argument and discussion through a mini enquiry session based on a philosophical question relating to the work of the day

- Display today's Big Question on the **CD (file 2.7)**:

  Should children be carers?

- Follow the process as explained at the end of Day 1 (p.112).

DAY 3

exploring the
meaning of words
in context

Word power 2 (CD)

Purpose: for children to develop their knowledge of and application of rarer vocabulary taken from the text and for children to understand how writers use language for effect

> dishevelled   tormenting   melancholy   anguish   domesticate

- Before the lesson, print the words and their synonyms from the **CD (file 3.1)** and display them on your word wall.
- Look at the words and their definitions on the **CD (file 3.2)** with the children and then read the sentences to them. Ask the children to repeat the sentences using MT/YT giving dramatic emphasis and actions as you say them.
- Tell the children that most of the language spoken by the characters is everyday spoken language but there are some words, especially those spoken by the elephant, that are not commonly used in everyday conversation.
- Find opportunities to use the words yourself during the day, e.g. 'I shall *domesticate* this class into tidying up!'
- Encourage the children use the words at home with friends and family so that they become embedded in their own spoken (and eventually, written) vocabulary.
- Now tell the children to do the Word power activity in the Pupils' Book p.43.

**Year 6
Grammar**
how hyphens can
be used to avoid
ambiguity

Grammar: hyphens to avoid confusion (CD) PB

Purpose: for children to develop their knowledge of when hyphens are used to avoid confusion and ambiguity

- Tell the children that in the play *The Elephant in the Room*, Caitlin describes Lina as a 'goodie-two-shoes'. Ask them to TTYP to come up with their own definition of what Caitlin meant by this adjective. Choose two or three sets of partners to share their definitions.

- Display **(CD file 3.3)** to show Caitlin's dialogue. Remind the children that the mark that looks like small dash in between each word is called a *hyphen*. Use MT/YT to say the word *hyphen*.
- Click 'Definition' to show the Oxford Junior Dictionary entry for hyphen. Read it out to the children.
- Say that hyphens can be used to join compound adjectives or compound nouns to avoid confusion.
- Click 'Next' to show examples and read both sentences aloud. Click 'TOL' and use the TOL bubble to draw attention to the potential for confusion.
- Navigate through the slides and repeat the process for the next two examples.
- Now ask the children to look at the Grammar: hyphens to avoid confusion activity on p.44 of their Pupils' Book. Explain the activity and ask them to complete it with their partners. Choose two to feed back on the first pair of sentences. Check their understanding and clarify if necessary. Repeat for the remaining pairs of sentences.

Homework Book p.17 provides further practice on using hyphens to avoid confusion.

Re-read a script version 3 🅰 ⒸⒹ

Curriculum link: checking that the play makes sense to them

Purpose: for children to gain a deeper understanding of the story and to see their own copy of the full text for the first time

- Let the children follow their own copy of the text in the Anthology p.54 as you re-play the full version of the play on the **CD (file 3.4)**. Explain that the Power words are in bold in the Anthology text.
- Now ask the children to read their copy of the script with their partners, taking one adult and one child part each, and to read the words and phrases in bold with great expression. Explain that you will be listening in.
- Tell the children to choose three parts of the script to 'freeze frame'. Explain that a freeze frame can be like a photograph – a snap shot of a particular moment in the play, e.g. they could freeze frame the moment when Caitlin asks Lina if she is going to the party, or when Mr Chang appears around the door, or when Lina thumps her books down because she is so cross.
- Remind them to think carefully about their body positions and their facial expressions. Who will they be looking at? What are they feeling inside?
- Give them time to practise their freeze frames and then select partners to show their freeze frames to the class.
- Ask the rest of the children to discuss what part of the script they might be framing.
- Now tell the class to all hold their freeze frames at the same time on a count of three.

What if not...? 🄿🄱

drawing inferences and justifying with evidence, identifying key details that support ideas

Purpose: for children to consider how character, setting and plot each affects the other

- Tell the children to look at the What if not...? questions in their Pupils' Books p.44. Model how you consider the first What if not...?: What if not *distrustful*? What if *Lina trusted Caitlin*? If Lina had told Caitlin about her father would she tease her? How would Lina's character change if she had a friend that she could share her worries with?
- Ask children to TTYP and discuss this and the other What if not...? questions in their Pupils' Books.

Daily log

Purpose: for children to keep a personal reading, writing and thinking log in order to record thoughts and ideas for their own writing

- Ask the children to record at least one more What if not...? in their Daily log with some notes about how the change might affect characters, plot and setting.

Big Question

Purpose: for children to develop their skills of argument and discussion through a mini enquiry session based on a philosophical question relating to the work of the day

- Display today's Big Question on the **CD (file 3.5)**:

  Do we always know what is best for us?

- Follow the process as explained at the end of Day 1 (p.112).

DAY 4

read silently

Re-read a script version 3

Purpose: for children to deepen their understanding of the script by increasing familiarity with the text

- Ask the children to read the whole script silently from the Anthology p.54. Tell them that they can stop to record any thoughts, ideas, questions or favourite bits in their Daily log as they read the text. Explain that it is more important for them to think about what they are reading than to finish first and, as they already know what happens, it doesn't matter if they don't finish this time.

drawing inferences
and justifying these
with evidence

What's explicit, what's implicit?

Purpose: for children to develop their ability to interpret text and sub-text

- Tell the children that the words on the page only give some of the story; to understand what characters might be thinking and what motivates them to act in particular ways we need to search for clues that might give us extra information.
- Explain that if the answer to a question draws on *explicit* information – you can find the answers in the text. If the answers require an answer that relies upon *implicit* information – you will have to work harder to answer these because the answer is not written down.
- Display the grid showing examples of explicit text from the script **CD (file 4.1)**. Model how you find the first example in the Anthology text. Discuss the first example with the children, explaining that often when someone is nervous they can't stand still and they pace. Tell the children that when things are out of control and you are worried it sometimes feels easier to blame someone else. You can tell Lina is upset but she doesn't say she is.
- Now guide the children to find the next example of text in the Anthology and TTYP to choose the most appropriate example of implicit text. Remind the children that they will need to justify their answers.
- Collect feedback and use drag and drop to complete the grid.
- Now tell the children to look at the What's explicit, what's implicit? activity in the Pupils' Book p.45 to explore the text. Remind the children that there is sometimes no correct answer to the questions, just their own carefully considered opinions.

Dramatic improvisation

Purpose: to understand the role of the elephant in the play

- Before you start this activity print off the 'emotion words' from the **CD (file 4.2)**. Cut them up into cards and shuffle them so they are in a random order for the improvisation.

- Tell the children that you are the elephant and you can control the mood of the room.
- Tell them you are going to call out 'emotion words' and they will react to them. The sad words make their movements heavy and small and the happy words help them straighten up and move more freely.
- The happy words have the opposite effect to the sad words on the elephant – the elephant relishes the sadness. Explain that if enough happy words are used together they will be able to banish the elephant, but if too many sad words are used they will curl up and be unable to move and the elephant will have won.
- Do the improvisation and afterwards take feedback asking the children how they felt as they shrank in on themselves.
- You may wish to display the 'emotion words' after the activity.

Curriculum link:
selecting
appropriate
vocabulary

Daily log

Purpose: for children to keep a personal reading, writing and thinking log in order to record thoughts and ideas for their own writing

- Tell the children to choose two contrasting 'emotion words' from the drama activity and make a mind map of synonyms for each of them.

effective
discussion; provide
justifications
for their views,
distinguish between
fact and opinion

Big Question

Purpose: for children to develop their skills of argument and discussion through a mini enquiry session based on a philosophical question relating to the work of the day

- Display today's Big Question on the **CD (file 4.3)**:

  Do we control how we feel?

- Follow the process as explained at the end of Day 1 (p.112).

DAY 5

describing
characters

Role on the wall

Purpose: for children to think more deeply about characters in the script and to record their ideas

- Before the lesson, print off a blank body outline for each set of partners from **CD (file 5.1)**.
- Display the body outline on the **CD (file 5.2)**. Explain that this represents the character of Lina and drag and drop her name into the body.
- Look at the characteristics bank and TOL as you select appropriate words to describe the character of Lina.
- Model using the Anthology text (p.54) to verify or disprove your choices.
- Draw the children into your TOL, encouraging them to disagree by deliberately making a 'wrong' choice. Don't make it look too easy. Model being unsure, change your mind and ask the children to TTYP to help you to choose.
- Drag and drop the chosen words and phrases into the body shape.
- Give the children the printouts of the blank body outlines and ask them to TTYP to complete at least one other role together for either Caitlin, Mr Chang or the elephant.
- Encourage the children to use their own words and phrases as well as the bank examples.
- Walk around as they talk and work, questioning choices and praising good partner work and choices.
- Ask partners to cut out their outlines and stick them up on the board or on a wall. Pick out similarities and differences in choices to stimulate further discussion. You could use the other names on the CD file to build up a Role on the wall for the other characters using children's feedback.

Drama

Curriculum link: identifying key details

Purpose: for children to use their knowledge of the characters to identify key moments of the action

- Summarise the knowledge the children have gathered about the characters from the last activity.
- Organise the children into groups of four (e.g. two sets of partners) so that they can act out the play. The child who plays Caitlin can double as the director. Ask them to act out the play.
- Stop the run through every five minutes and ask each group to TTYP and discuss how their character is feeling at that moment. Take feedback and encourage the children to decide if that moment in the play is important for their character.
- Once they have completed a run-through ask the children to TTYP and discuss which points in the play were highly emotional or important to the development of their character. Take feedback.

Daily log

noting ideas

Purpose: for children to keep a personal reading, writing and thinking log in order to record thoughts and ideas for their own writing

- Tell the children to note down in their Daily log three things they found out about the character they acted in the play.

Big Question

effective discussion; provide justifications for their views

Purpose: for children to develop their skills of argument and discussion through a mini enquiry session based on a philosophical question relating to the work of the day

- Display today's Big Question on the **CD (file 5.3)**:

  What is the hardest thing that could be asked of you?

- Follow the process as explained at the end of Day 1 (p.112).

WRITING FICTION

Build a character

understand, through being shown, the skills and processes essential for writing

Purpose: for children to be able to use details to begin to build a character

- Tell the children that you want to create a character for a script you are thinking of writing. It is a character to replace the elephant in the room. This new character will represent guilt.
- Ask the children to TTYP to explore what guilt feels like. Take feedback.
- Explain that in the play we have read the elephant was invisible to the other characters but he controlled them at times. If you felt guilty it could control your actions. Tell the children that you are going to use the role on the wall figure to record some words and phrases that will tell us more about this controlling character.
- Display the **CD (file 6.1)** to show the blank role on the wall figure, the bank of words and phrases and character statements.
- Read the statements and ask the children to help you to find one or more words or phrases that could match up with the statement. Drag and drop into the figure, e.g.

  It appears whenever people have got something they want to hide.

  word/phrase: feeding on weaknesses, unsympathetic, parasitic.

- Encourage the children to offer synonyms for the chosen words.

Show, don't tell ⓒ ᴾᴮ

Curriculum link: considering how authors develop character

Purpose: for children to explore ways of developing characterisation by showing, rather than telling

- Explain that the character statements *tell* us what the character has done and the words inside the figure *tell* us what kind of person it is, but you are now going to write a sentence that will *show* us what the character is like.
- Click on **CD (file 6.2)** to display the beginning of the process of developing one of the statements into a *telling* and then a *showing* sentence.
- Say the sentence: 'The elephant appears in the room snickering, moving close so he can feed off their guilt.' and then TOL about what this would really look like:

  If I was an actor and I wanted to show the elephant appearing in the room I would **slide in from off stage** and direct my attention to the guilty looking characters. **I would rub my hands with glee** and **snicker with delight** as **I sidle up to them** and **stand close to them,** overshadowing them.

  Mime the actions, stance, body language, and facial expressions of the elephant.

- Ask the children to do their own mime. Ask them to freeze-frame. Walk round commenting, using appropriate and varied vocabulary to describe what you see.
- Click on **CD (file 6.3)** to display words and the rest of the process of developing the *telling* sentence into a *showing* sentence.
- Now ask the children to look at the *telling* sentence in their Pupils' Books p.46 and TTYP to discuss how to turn it into two or three *showing* sentences.
- When all the children have their opening sentence ready, ask them to write it down.
- Collect feedback and scribe some good examples on the board or a flipchart.

Build a speech ⓒ

understand, through being shown, the skills and processes essential for writing

Purpose: for children to revise the conventions of writing speech in a script

- Remind the children that the elephant is going to be a character in a playscript representing guilt.
- Explain that only the audience and the main character can hear the elephant's words, as he is the main character's guilty conscience.
- Display the Doing, feeling, thinking or saying grid on the **CD (file 6.4)**.
- TOL as you go through the two examples, drawing the children into the TOL and offering your own variations or additions.
- Now complete the rest of the grid as a whole class task, use TTYP and feedback, scribing responses using the writing tool.

Daily log

noting ideas

Purpose: for children to keep a personal reading, writing and thinking log in order to record thoughts and ideas for their own writing

- Ask the children to think of a situation where a child might feel guilty. Tell them to record one of the ideas in note form in their Daily log.

Big Question ⓒ

effective discussion; provide justifications for their views

Purpose: for children to develop their skills of argument and discussion through a mini enquiry session based on a philosophical question relating to the work of the day

- Display today's Big Question on the **CD (file 6.5)**:

  Which is worse: the guilt or the secret?

- Follow the process as explained at the end of Day I (p.112).

DAY 7

Curriculum link:
describing
atmosphere

Dramatic improvisation

Purpose: for children to explore the central theme of their writing

- Display the image of Banksy's *Elephant in the Room* on the **CD (file 7.1)** and ask the children to TTYP and discuss their reaction to it, especially in response to the play they have been exploring.
- Ask the children to imagine they are in the room with the elephant and TTYP to discuss what it would feel like having to ignore such a huge presence.
- Tell the children to work in their pairs miming being the elephant in the room overshadowing the person in the room. Give them time to take both parts. Take feedback about how it felt ignoring the elephant.
- Now re-play the improvisation but with the elephant muttering about the main character's guilty secret, making the other person feel more guilty and awful.
- Collect feedback and scribe some good examples on the board or a flipchart.

understand,
through being
shown, the skills
and processes
essential for writing

Build a script 1

Purpose: for children to be able to see a script grow through three stages of development

- Remind the children that they heard two versions of *The Elephant in the Room* (Script versions 1 & 2) before they heard and read the full script. It prepared them to read the full script.
- Explain that you are going to show them two versions of the first scene of a new script to be written. These versions prepared the writer to write the full script of the first scene. Show the writer's statements on the **CD (file 7.2)** and explain that these were the prompts that helped the writer to know what to put in the new script. Take the role of writer for these activities.
- Now display Build a script 1 on the **CD (file 7.3)**.
- Read out loud to the children. Explain that you are now going to show them another version of the first scene of the new script to be written. This one has additional information and words – it has been developed.

making
comparisons

Build a script 2

Purpose: for children to be able to see a script grow through three stages of development

- Show Build a script 2 on the **CD (file 7.4)**. TOL as you compare this version with Build a script 1. Click on the 'Highlights' icon to show additional information, synonyms and descriptive language.

using similar
writing as models
for their own

Build a script 3

Purpose: for children to see an example of writing that will provide a model for their own writing

- An example script is provided as a model for writing. Remain in the role of the writer of this script during these activities.
- Display the script on the **CD (file 7.5)**. Explain that when writing this script, your purpose was to entertain and interest the audience or reader and also to start them guessing what Geeta's problem might be.
- Read Build a script 3 to the children.

noting ideas,
provide
justifications for
their views

Daily log

Purpose: for children to keep a personal reading, writing and thinking log in order to record thoughts and ideas for their own writing

- Ask the children to share ideas for a title for the script. Ask them to record their best idea in their Daily log and explain why they think it is a good title.

Curriculum link:
effective
discussion; provide
justifications for
their views

Big Question

*Purpose: for children to develop their skills of argument and discussion through a mini
enquiry session based on a philosophical question relating to the work of the day*

- Display today's Big Question on the **CD (file 7.6)**:

  Is there ever a good time to lie?

- Follow the process as explained at the end of Day 1 (p.112).

DAY 8

assessing the
effectiveness of
others' writing

Evaluation

*Purpose: for children to develop their ability to evaluate the effectiveness of a piece
of writing*

- Print out copies of Build a script 3 from the **CD (file 8.1)**. Ask the children to
  TTYP to read the script together. Each child should take two parts – whichever
  partner reads Dad's part will also read the stage directions.
- Using TTYP and oral feedback, ask the children to evaluate the writing using
  the guide questions in the Pupils' Book p.46. Collect feedback and encourage
  discussion and constructive argument.

plan their writing

Write a script 1

Purpose: to develop children's confidence and skills in script planning and development

- Explain that you are going to guide the children in planning what happens next in
  the play.
- Display Facts and questions on the **CD (file 8.2)**. Encourage the children to
  TTYP and discuss the possible answers to the questions. Take feedback and
  discuss possible scenarios.
- Tell the children to jot down the answers to the questions in their Daily log as
  they will need them later.
- Model how to add detail to the plan for the next two scenes on the **CD (file 8.3)**
  (this can be printed off from **CD (file 8.4)** for the children to plan with).
- Now ask the children to TTYP and discuss the prompts on the planner. Take
  feedback, relating their ideas to the planning structure.
- Ask the children to write their own plan.

using similar
writing as models
for their own

Write a script 2

Purpose: to develop children's confidence and skills in script planning and development

- Using TOL, and encouraging the children to offer their ideas, model how to
  develop the elephant's speech on the **CD (file 8.5)** by dragging and dropping
  phrases into his taunt.
- Now navigate through the screens and click 'TOL' to expand the sentence using
  the speech bubbles on the CD. Display the final sentences.
- Ask the children to read the bare bones of the elephant's final speech in the Pupil's
  Book p.47 and write their own developed version in their Daily log.
- Now TOL about stage directions and model the conventions of writing them in
  a script. Model writing the elephant's speech with extra stage directions showing
  when and where he moves.

Curriculum link:
writing dialogue

Daily log

Purpose: for children to keep a personal reading, writing and thinking log in order to record thoughts and ideas for their own writing

- Ask the children to write Geeta's response to the elephant's final speech. Does it make her tell her secret or does it defeat her? If she tells, what are the consequences? Ask the children to write notes in their Daily log.

effective discussion; provide justifications for their views

Big Question

Purpose: for children to develop their skills of argument and discussion through a mini enquiry session based on a philosophical question relating to the work of the day

- Display today's Big Question on the **CD (file 8.6)**:

  What would persuade you to do something you were very scared of? *

- Follow the process as explained at the end of Day 1 (p.112).

* This Big Question will be revisited on Day 11 – the first day of the non-fiction week (p.125).

DAY 9

Write a script 3 📘

Purpose: for children to use the speeches and stage directions they have already developed to continue and finish the play

write by selecting appropriate vocabulary, understanding how such choices can enhance meaning

- Tell the children that they are now ready to write the rest of the play. Remind them that it should: use monologue, have only one setting for the action and have all the action take place in one scene, and include stage directions.
- Ask them to use the 'Remember to:' prompts in the Pupils' Books p.47. Remind them to use any useful parts of their Daily log to help them and to look at the word wall for Power words and phrases and a thesaurus for synonyms.
- Encourage children to rehearse their opening sentence with their partners before they begin to write.
- Remind them of the speeches you modelled in class, but encourage them to use their own ideas, add more speeches between characters and think of a suitable ending to the scene.

DAY 10

Share a script

Purpose: for children to read and share their playscripts

assessing the effectiveness of their own and others' writing

- Ask the children to read through their own playscripts.
- Now tell them to re-read their episode and underline their favourite or best parts. Ask them to share these with their partners and even act parts out to see how they work. Collect feedback on best bits from partners.
- Make sure that any powerful words or phrases are written on cards and added to the word wall.

Evaluate and edit ⓒⒹ

Purpose: for children to evaluate their own and their partner's work against specific criteria and then discuss how they could improve their work

- Display **CD (file 10.1)** to show the evaluation prompts and read them together using MT/YT.
- As a model, select an example of work from the children where the writing has met the criteria, and share this with the other children, explaining why it works well.
- Tell the children to take turns to read their partner's writing and discuss how well they have met the criteria.

- Ask children to discuss at least two changes they could make to improve their work following the partner discussion.

Curriculum link: proofread for spelling and punctuation errors

Proofread

Purpose: for children to proofread their work and make changes to improve the accuracy of their grammar, punctuation and spelling

- Now ask the children to proofread their work. If you have noticed that several children need to improve on a particular aspect of spelling, grammar or punctuation, use this as a focus for the Proofread activity. Write an example which includes common errors from the children's writing and use this as a model.
- The children should always be checking for standard use of punctuation and correct spelling of common exception words.
- The following points would be relevant as the particular focus for this Unit:
  - check that playscript conventions have been used correctly, e.g. stage directions and scene descriptions
  - check spelling of ambitious vocabulary choices.

effective discussion; provide justifications for their views, distinguish between fact and opinion

Very Big Question

Purpose: for children to develop their willingness to broaden or revise their opinions through exploring one of the Big Questions in more depth

- See Unit 1 Day 10 for teaching notes on the Very Big Question p.36.

Persuasive texts

READING AND WRITING NON-FICTION

In the non-fiction part of the Unit persuasive texts are studied, looking at biased articles, advertorials and adverts. Children write a scripted presentation which includes persuasive techniques such as rhetorical questions, pre-empting and exaggeration. They use it to persuade the class to vote either for or against the use of a brain boosting memory aid in schools.

See p.108 for the daily timetable for the Non-fiction week.

Non-fiction

Reading

Children will:

- explore different types of persuasive texts
- think about the different techniques that writers can use to persuade the reader
- identify bias in a persuasive text and understand how it can be created
- distinguish fact and opinion in persuasive texts.

Writing

Key writing purpose to be shared with the children:

To write a persuasive presentation about whether 'Memoraid' should or should not be used in schools.

Writing evaluation to be shared with the children

My persuasive presentation:

- has a clear introduction, three main ideas and a conclusion
- addresses the audience directly
- uses persuasive techniques, e.g. *rhetorical questions, pre-empts, exaggeration.*

Grammar:

- uses punctuation correctly for effect, e.g. exclamation marks, question marks.

See the Planning section of the Software ('Timetables' tab) for a printable version of the Writing purpose and evaluation.

DAY 11

Curriculum link: learn the conventions of different types of writing

Introduction

Purpose: for children to revise their existing knowledge of persuasive texts using the context of one of the Big Questions and the scripts studied in weeks 1 and 2

- Display the Big Question from Day 8 on the **CD (file 8.6)**: *What would persuade you to do something you were very scared of?*
- Review the discussion the children had about this Big Question and draw their attention to how we are persuaded to do and buy things every day.
- Ask the children to TTYP and discuss the different ways in which they are persuaded. Take feedback, noting the difference in the types of persuasion from 'in your face' adverts to the more subtle way of persuading people.
- Ask the children to TTYP and discuss times when they have tried to persuade their parents or carers to do or buy something. How did they try to do it? Take feedback and note down the children's strategies, asking if they were successful or not.
- Review the information so far, for example parents can be persuaded to do and buy things by their children if they believe it is good for the children, their child will feel left out if they don't have it, everyone would benefit in some way or simply because they are worn down!
- Now ask the children to TTYP and discuss how they are persuaded to want the things they pester their parents for. Take feedback.
- Tell the children that you are going to investigate the power of persuasive writing.

exploring the meaning of words in context

Word power

Purpose: for children to become familiar with some words and synonyms associated with persuasive texts

> opinion   biased   logical   rhetorical question   pre-empt   elaborate   convince

- Ask the children to look at the words and sentences in their Pupils' Books p.48. Explain that they are all words we use when we talk about persuasive texts.
- Now read the sentences to the children. Ask the children to repeat the sentences using MT/YT.
- Before the lesson, print the words and their definitions from the **CD (file 11.1)** and display them on your persuasion word wall.
- Find opportunities to use the words yourself during the day, e.g. 'I love this book, but I am *biased!*; Can you *elaborate* on what you were thinking there?; I'm going to *pre-empt* the bell and let you out early!' and encourage the children to use them in their everyday conversation.
- Now ask Partner 1s to read the word and its meaning and Partner 2s to read the sentences containing the word.

retrieve information from non-fiction

Bias

Purpose: for children to be able to recognise bias in a persuasive text

- Display the persuasive text on the **CD (file 11.2)** and read it aloud to the children. TOL to summarise what the text is about, i.e. *MORF, a memory trainer*.
- Say that this article is extremely biased. Bias can be created using put downs, exaggeration and by stating as fact things that can't be easily proven.
- Ask the children to TTYP and discuss the evidence that MORF works. Take feedback, discussing whether this proof has real scientific evidence.

- Click 'Highlights' to show areas of the text which demonstrate put down, exaggeration and facts without provable evidence. TOL to explore what is revealed and the effect that each strategy might have on the reader.
- Ask the children to TTYP and discuss which of the strategies is the most effective in creating bias. Take feedback.

Curriculum link: distinguish between fact and opinion

Fact vs opinion PB

Purpose: for children to be able to identify the difference between fact and opinion

- Tell the children that persuasive texts often try to hide opinion, hearsay or unproven ideas as fact by using phrases such as 'Many scientists say…' 'It is thought…' 'It is reported…' These cunning words hide the truth – that the facts and ideas are unproven, exaggerations or hide most of the truth.
- Ask the children to look at the texts in their Pupils' Book pp.49–50. Read each text out loud to them.
- Ask them take turns to read each text and TTYP to identify the facts and opinions in the texts. Tell them to look out for the cunning words that are used to hide the opinions, exaggerations and half-truths.
- Collect feedback and use TOL as necessary when you clarify.

Daily log PB

Purpose: for children to keep a personal reading, writing and thinking log in order to record thoughts and ideas for their own writing

- Tell the children to try and change two factual sentences from the texts in the Pupils' Books p.50 into opinions.

DAY 12

Deconstruction 1 A

Purpose: for children to see an example of writing that will provide a model for the planning of their own writing

retrieve information from non-fiction, provide justifications for their views

- Ask the children to follow as you read 'Make memory lapses a thing to forget' in the Anthology p.66.
- Summarise that it is about a brain trainer called *Memoraid* and that it is a form of advertising called an advertorial, where information is given about a product as if it is an article written by the magazine or newspaper in which it appears.
- Ask the children to TTYP to find evidence of bias and exaggeration in this advertorial. Take feedback.
- Draw the children's attention to the quotes from satisfied customers. Ask the children to TTYP and discuss whether or not they trust these testimonials. Take feedback and then decide as a class whether or not this information can be trusted. Encourage the children to give reasons and evidence for their opinions.

learn the conventions of different types of writing

Read a persuasive text CD A 🖨

Purpose: for children to understand and locate examples of the key features of a persuasive text

- Display the Checklist for key features of persuasive texts grid on the **CD (file 12.1)** and TOL as you find examples of each feature in 'Make memory lapses a thing to forget' in the Anthology p.66.
- Tell the children to work with their partners to complete their own grids. They can be printed from **CD (file 12.2)** for children to record their answers on.
- Collect answers and use the completed grid on the CD to clarify points and show different examples.

DAY 13

Curriculum link:
discuss their
understanding of
what they have
read

Deconstruction 2

Purpose: for children to read and identify the persuasive techniques used in an advert

- Ask the children to take turns to read the advert for *Memoraid* in the Anthology p.67 exaggerating the ridiculous claims and persuasive language with their voices. Point out the high number of question marks as the advertiser tries to engage the reader, and of exclamation marks for some of the wilder claims of the advert.
- Ask the children to TTYP and identify all the persuasive techniques used in this advert. Take feedback.
- Tell the children that sometimes pre-empts are used in persuasion. They address an obvious concern or area of weakness before it can be used to discredit the positive aspects of the product or idea that is being put forward.
- Display **CD (file 13.1)** and click 'Reveal' to show the first *Concern, Response* and *Pre-empt*. TOL to show how the pre-empt is written with a positive spin.
- Show the next concern and response and ask the children to TTYP and compose their own pre-empt. Take feedback exploring particularly positive pre-empts and then share the pre-empt on the CD.
- Show the final concern. Ask the children to TTYP to discuss the possible responses and then to compose their own pre-empts. Take feedback and allow the children time to write their favourite pre-empts in their Daily log.

perform their own
compositions

Role-play

Purpose: for children to manipulate a persuasive text for effect

- Tell the children that Swindles Direct have commissioned a 30-second radio advert and that they need to work in groups of four to create one.
- Tell the children to use the Memoraid advert in the Anthology p.67 as the starting point. Explain that they need to talk directly to the audience, compose a memorable slogan or jingle and decide on the most important thing to say about Memoraid.
- Give them time to plan their advert and have a quick run through before presenting to the class.
- Discuss which adverts worked well and how others could be improved.

evaluate how
authors use
language,
considering the
impact on the
reader

Improve a persuasive text [PB]

Purpose: for children to use persuasive language to improve a persuasive text

- Ask the children to look at the opening of a persuasive text in the Pupils' Book p.51.
- Remind them how the pre-empts tried hard to present any problems in a positive light.
- Draw their attention to the first sentence 'Memoraid is really nice and helps you remember stuff' and model how it can be changed to 'Memoraid is an amazing memory trainer!' which presents a much more punchy positive picture.
- Tell the children they can improve the text by: 1) Addressing the audience directly. 2) Using simple psychology to appeal to the audience's judgement (i.e. making them feel clever if they agree with you). 3) Choosing strong positive words and phrases.
- Ask them to improve the text orally and then write their improvements into their Daily log.

DAY 14

plan their writing

Deconstruction 3

Purpose: for children to explore how to plan and order their ideas within a persuasive text

- Tell children that they are going to be writing a persuasive presentation about Memoraid and they will choose to either support its use in schools or oppose it. They will need to persuade the class that their point of view is right.

- Display the planning grid on the **CD (file 14.1)**, and explain that the opening statement of their persuasive presentation will need to capture the audience's attention. Type your opening statement into the box provided, introducing your persuasive presentation.
- Navigate to the next screen, drag and drop the ideas *against* Memoraid into the grid and type an argument *for* into the final column (you will need to use the *Enter* key to move down to the next box). TOL, using the persuasive phrases to compose a possible first sentence.
- Ask children to TTYP and compose their first sentence. Take feedback.
- Repeat this for all three paragraphs. Explain to the children that you have provided examples for both sides of the argument but that they will need to decide whether they are going to argue for or against Memoraid.
- Explain that the order of the paragraphs can affect the power of the argument. Ask children to suggest changes that could be made to the order of the paragraphs.
- Navigate to the final screen and TOL to model how you sum up and reiterate in the closing statement.
- Ask children to choose if they want to write their persuasive presentation for or against the sale of Memoraid to school children. Give the children printouts of the blank planning grid from the **CD (file 14.2)** before you begin this activity. Tell them to use the planner to plan their writing. Remind children that they will need to think about which phrases to use depending on whether they have decided to argue for or against Memoraid.

> **Curriculum link:** continue to write for a range of purposes and audiences

Write to persuade PB

Purpose: for children to use their planning and notes to help them to write a persuasive presentation

- Tell the children that they are going to write a short persuasive presentation. Some partners will be chosen to deliver their presentations to the class. It will have an introduction, three main ideas and a conclusion.
- Remind the children about the persuasive techniques that they have explored and tell them to use their plan and writing prompts in the Pupils' Book, p.51 to help them.
- Tell them to make sure that they have a pre-empt that changes a negative point into a positive point.

> proofread for spelling and punctuation errors

Proofread

Purpose: for children to proofread their work and make changes to improve the accuracy of their grammar, punctuation and spelling

- Now ask the children to proofread their work. If you have noticed that several children need to improve on a particular aspect of spelling, grammar or punctuation, use this as a focus for the Proofread activity. Write an example which includes common errors from the children's writing and use this as a model.
- The children should always be checking for standard use of punctuation and correct spelling of common exception words.
- The following points would be relevant as the particular focus for this Unit:
  - check for correct use of punctuation for effect, e.g. exclamation marks and question marks
  - check that capital letters are used for proper nouns.

DAY 15

Curriculum link:
perform their own
compositions

Persuasive presentations

Purpose: for children to complete and present their persuasive arguments for or against the sale of Memoraid to school children

- Allow time for the children to complete their presentation notes.
- Tell the children that they are going to present as if they were at a committee meeting.
- Remind them about respecting each other's points of view and listening carefully to each other.
- Take the role of the neutral chairperson to 'open' the meeting and to chair it as the selected partners deliver their persuasive presentations in turn.
- At the end of all the presentations, tell the children that they are going to vote for or against allowing Memoraid to be sold to school children. Make sure they know that they can change their original views if they have been persuaded by other people's arguments.

record information

Daily log

Purpose: for children to keep a personal reading, writing and thinking log in order to record thoughts and ideas for their own writing

- Ask the children to vote and then record the *fact* of the result in their Daily log with a brief note on their *opinion* of the result.

assessing the
effectiveness of
their own and
others' writing

Evaluate and edit

Purpose: for children to evaluate their own and their partner's work against specific criteria and then discuss how they could improve their work

- Display **CD (file 15.1)** to show the evaluation prompts and read them together using MT/YT.
- As a model, select an example of a presentation where the children met the criteria, and share with the other children why it worked well.
- Tell the children to discuss with their partner how well they met the criteria.
- Ask children to discuss at least two changes they could make to improve their presentation following the partner discussion.

Fiction: Authors and texts
Non-fiction: Explanations

Timetable

WEEK 1   **Reading fiction**   **Authors and texts –** *I Believe in Unicorns*

Day 1	Day 2	Day 3	Day 4	Day 5
The story store	Read a story version 3	Word power 🖨	Re-read a story version 3	Who says?
Read a story version 1	Clarify	Read a story version 3	Zoom in on sentence types	Daily log: Drama
Think and link	Think and link story map	Read and compare 🖨	Drama	Daily log
Read a story version 2	Daily log	Daily log	Daily log	What if not...?
Daily log	Big Question	Big Question	Big Question	Daily log
Big Question				Big Question

WEEK 2   **Writing fiction**   **Authors and texts –** *I Believe in Unicorns*

Day 6	Day 7	Day 8	Day 9	Day 10
Build a sentence 🖨	Grammar: linking ideas across paragraphs	Write a story 1	Write a story 3	Share a story
Tell a story	Build a setting	Role-play – Lost!		Evaluate and edit
Daily log	Plan a story	Write a story 2 🖨		Proofread
Big Question	Build an episode	Daily log		Very Big Question
	Daily log	Big Question		
	Big Question			

WEEK 3   **Reading and writing non-fiction**   Explanations

Day 11	Day 12	Day 13	Day 14	Day 15
Linking the texts	Deconstruction 1	Deconstruction 2	Deconstruction 3	Evaluate and edit
Introduction	Read an explanation 🖨	Build an explanation – plan 🖨	Write an explanation	Proofread
Instructions and explanations	Daily log	Daily log		Presentation
Audience				
Daily log				

🖨: shows that a file should be printed out from the Software.

Overview of the Unit

This Unit explores the work of Michael Morpurgo using *I Believe in Unicorns* as the central text. The children will explore Morpurgo's themes and style of writing as well as analysing how he creates atmosphere, character and imagery. By the end of this Unit the children will have worked in role as the central character and composed a multi-layered text, which supports their narrative writing.

In the non-fiction part of the Unit children examine the explanation text 'How does a story become a Manga graphic novel?' and write their own explanation text on a book-based theme. For more information about the Non-fiction week and the Non-fiction writing evaluation criteria, see p.146.

The Homework Book provides a homework activity related to the content of this Unit for each of the three weeks.

Fiction

Reading

Children will:

- explore the themes in Michael Morpurgo's writing, and connect these to the themes in *I Believe in Unicorns*
- explore how Michael Morpurgo uses different sentence types to create imagery and atmosphere
- consider the viewpoints of the different characters in the story.

Writing

Key writing purpose to be shared with the children:

To write a new episode for the story, exploring how Tomas would feel if he became separated from his parents during the conflict in the city.

Writing evaluation to be shared with the children

My story:

- includes thoughts and feelings which develop what we know about Tomas as he reacts to new events
- includes an incident and a resolution in the new episode
- uses all of the senses to describe vividly the bombed town.

Grammar:

- uses cohesive devices to link ideas across paragraphs, e.g. *repetition*, *adverbials* and *pronouns*
- uses first person and past tense to tell the story from Tomas' point of view.

See the Planning section of the Software ('Timetables' tab) for a printable version of the Writing purpose and evaluation.

Fiction: Authors and texts

I Believe in Unicorns by Michael Morpurgo

READING FICTION

DAY 1

Curriculum link:
identifying and discussing themes and conventions, making comparisons across stories

Resources

PB Pupils' Book, pp.52–64

A Anthology, pp.68–80

CD CD on interactive whiteboard (Unit 6)

GB Grammar Bank on CD

HB Homework Book, pp.20–23

The story store (CD)

Purpose: to understand who Michael Morpurgo is and contextualise the main themes of his work

- It would be a good idea to make a Michael Morpurgo book corner to support this Unit and to give the children access to his work. More about the author, including lots of biographical information and summaries of his work, as well as a links to interviews and articles, can be found on his website.
- Use the mind map on the **CD (file 1.1)** to brainstorm any prior knowledge the children have of Michael Morpurgo's books. Read some of the titles of his books and show the front covers. Ask the children to TTYP (Turn to your partner) and discuss their initial impression of his books.
- Display the summaries of three of his short stories on the **CD (file 1.2)**.
- Draw the children's attention to the themes of the stories. Break down one of the story summaries so that they can see how Morpurgo explores ideas and themes that are sometimes tricky to talk about. Note that his writing can be quite emotive, i.e. his books are designed to make the reader feel emotions keenly.
- Ask the children to TTYP and discuss the themes of the stories in the story store. Is there one main theme that stands out as common to all the stories?
- Introduce the concept of using the past to make a comment on the present. Discuss how the theme of secrets being lies is used to express a historical truth about the secret of the concentration camp and then as a specific example of Paulo refusing to speak of a difficult memory for him and so keeping it secret. Morpurgo is exploring the idea that secrecy can be dangerous and can be a lie disguised by another name.
- Display one of the summaries and ask the children to TTYP and discuss why giving up the past might be difficult.
- Return to the mind map on the **CD (file 1.1)** and add some information about the themes of Michael Morpurgo's writing.

read a range of fiction

Read a story version 1 (CD)

Purpose: for children to become familiar with Story version 1; the bare bones of I Believe in Unicorns

- Read Story version 1 aloud to the children. (Do not reveal the ending.)
  1. A boy goes to the library and hears a wonderful story.
  2. The storyteller tells the story sitting on a carved unicorn.
  3. Some of the children tell stories too. The boy wants to but is too shy.
  4. The boy tells his friends about the incredible storyteller and they come along to the library too.
  5. The storyteller tells the children about a time when she was a child and her father saved a book.
  6. One day the boy tells a story too.
  7. Then the valley is invaded.
  8. The library is hit by bombs and is on fire.

- Use MT/YT (My turn/Your turn) and TTYP for each point – you will need to break down the longer points. Use exaggerated intonation and emphasis where appropriate. This is to help the children to hold the basic story in their heads.
- Now display Story version 1 on the **CD (file 1.3)** so the children can see the text and note how much of it they have remembered.

Curriculum link: discussing themes

Think and link

Purpose: for children to make links and connections with other Michael Morpurgo stories

- Return to the Story store on the **CD (file 1.2)** and make links between these stories and Story version 1(e.g. *the way the past links with the present*).
- Ask the children to TTYP and discuss if they can see any themes emerging in the story (e.g. *books, fire, storytelling*).
- Draw the children's attention to the unicorn and ask them to TTYP and think about why it is important in the story.

predicting; identifying how language and structure contribute to meaning

Read a story version 2

Purpose: for children to examine how Story version 2 provides additional information for the reader and for children to become more familiar with the story before they hear the full version

- Read Story version 2 to the children.
  1. One day Tomas Porec goes unwillingly to the library, whilst his mother goes shopping. To his surprise, he is captivated by a wonderful story about unicorns.
  2. Expectant children surround the storyteller as she tells the story sitting on a carved unicorn. Amazed, he listens as the children take their turns and tell stories sitting on the unicorn as well.
  3. Tomas tells his friends about the unicorn lady and word spreads until a whole crowd of children come to hear and tell stories on the unicorn.
  4. One afternoon the unicorn lady takes a blackened book from her bag and tells the children about a time when she was a child and her father saved this book from the fire.
  5. She asks Tomas to read the book and he too reads on the unicorn. Suddenly he is not afraid and he makes the words dance on the air.
  6. Then one summer morning, tanks and soldiers invade the valley.
  7. Tomas and his father hide until it is safe and return to the town to see the library has been hit by bombs and is on fire.
- Now display this version on the **CD (file 1.4)**. Click 'Highlights' to show how the story has been developed. Point out the description, names, links to the past, and repeated images to the children.
- TOL and use TTYP to share how this extra information changes the pictures in our minds as we hear the story. Link what they have read and heard so far with the themes of Michael Morpurgo's writing.
- Hide the text and ask the children to use TTYP and take turns telling the story to each other one section at a time.
- Ask the children to work in pairs and discuss the questions in the Pupils' Book p.52

predicting what might happen

Daily log

Purpose: for children to make a prediction about the story ending

- Ask the children to think about how the story might end and to write down their prediction in their Daily log.

Curriculum link: effective discussion; provide justifications for their views

Big Question (CD)

Purpose: for children to develop their deeper thinking skills through a mini enquiry session based on a philosophical question relating to the work of the day

- Display today's Big Question on the **CD (file 1.5)**.

  Are secrets lies by another name?

- Ask the children to TTYP to discuss. Collect feedback from partners and scribe some responses. Tell the children that each day's Big Question and their thoughts will be collected and saved so that at the end of week 2 they can then vote on which question to discuss more deeply. See Introduction for further notes (p.13).

DAY 2

explain and discuss their understanding of what they have read

Read a story version 3

Purpose: for children to hear and enjoy the full version of the story for the first time

- Tell the children they are now going to hear the whole story for the very first time. TOL about which parts you are looking forward to hearing.
- Read the full story from the Anthology p.68 to the children with great enjoyment and appropriate intonation. Make your storytelling a performance and try to enhance Michael Morpurgo's imagery and layered themes.
- Make links to the predictions the children made in their Daily log. Ask the children to TTYP to share their predictions. Discuss the link with imagery created by the fire at the library and the fire from which the unicorn lady's father saved *The Little Match Girl*.

Clarify (CD)

Purpose: for children to link the story to their understanding of Michael Morpurgo's style

- Go through the story using TOL to identify some obvious examples of Michael Morpurgo's style. Use the text on the **CD (file 2.1)**. Click 'TOL' to reveal the think bubbles.
- Afterwards ask the children to TTYP and discuss how the unicorn image is used throughout the story. Take feedback.

summarising the main ideas

Think and link story map (CD)

Purpose: for children to understand the chronology and main points of the story

- Reveal the story map on the **CD (file 2.2)** and go through it using TOL to discuss the main events of the story. Draw the children's attention to the flashback to the past when the unicorn lady talks about her father saving the book from the fire.

identifying key details

Daily log (CD)

Purpose: for children to create a written or drawn representation of the story that can be used as an aide memoire

- Ask the children to map the story – you may wish to display **CD (file 2.2)** for support. Encourage them to add details, especially of the ending and the flashback.

effective discussion; provide justifications for their views

Big Question (CD)

Purpose: for children to develop their skills of argument and discussion through a mini enquiry session based on a philosophical question relating to the work of the day

- Display today's Big Question on the **CD (file 2.3)**:

  What is the value of a book?

- Follow the process as explained at the end of Day 1 (at the top of the page).

DAY 3

Curriculum link: exploring the meaning of words in context

Word power

Purpose: for children to visualise strong descriptive phrases and think about how they help the reader engage with a story

> spinning   jostling   longed   entranced   plucked   danced   blasting and shooting
> staggering   smudged and blackened   a weaver of tales

- Display the Power words on the **CD (file 3.1)**.
- Drag the phrases into the focus box and TOL describing the images and ideas these words give about the setting to you as a reader. Make connections with the text and link the phrases clearly with the images you are creating whilst reading. For example: 'Every story she told us held us entranced.' The word entranced makes me feel that she has the children in a spell. I can imagine the children sitting cross-legged and totally transfixed. This adds to the magical quality that the author has given the unicorn and the unicorn lady.
- You may wish to print off the words from the **CD (file 3.2)** and display them on the story wall.

checking that the story makes sense to them

Read a story version 3

Purpose: for children to gain a deeper understanding of the story and to see the text for the first time

- Let the children see and follow their own copy of the text in the Anthology p.68 as you re-read the full version of the story aloud to them with enthusiasm, enjoyment and appropriate intonation. Place special emphasis upon the Power words in bold and stop at the special phrases so that the children can "jump in". See Introduction for further explanation (p.13).
- Now ask the children to read their copy of the story with their partners, alternate sections each. Ask them to read together any words and phrases in bold with great expression. Explain that you will be listening in on readings.

making comparisons within and across books

Read and compare

Purpose: for children to compare and contrast the openings of stories by the same author.

- Print out copies of the chart from the **CD (file 3.3)** for the children to share one between two.
- Read the opening two paragraphs of *The Mozart Question* on the **CD (file 3.5)** to the children.
- Now display the chart on the **CD (file 3.4)**. Click 'Complete' to show the notes for *The Mozart Question*. Use TOL to note the character, verb tense, setting, hook and other details.
- Display the next text on the **CD (file 3.5)** and do the same for this text. Take feedback and add it to the key features chart.
- Repeat with the opening of the third text.
- Finally, ask the children to read the opening first two paragraphs of *I Believe in Unicorns* in their Anthology Books p.68 and complete the chart.

identifying themes

Daily log

Purpose: for children to make links between the stories

- Ask the children to write some notes in their Daily log about a theme that links two or three of the books together.

Curriculum link:
effective
discussion; provide
justifications for
their views

Big Question CD

Purpose: for children to develop their skills of argument and discussion through a mini enquiry session based on a philosophical question relating to the work of the day

- Display today's Big Question on the **CD (file 3.6)**:

  Does it matter if we believe in things that are not real?

- Follow the process as explained at the end of Day 1 (p.134).

DAY 4

Re-read a story version 3

read silently

Purpose: for children to deepen their understanding of a story by increasing familiarity with the text

- Ask the children to read the whole story silently from the Anthology p.68. Tell them that they can stop to record any thoughts, ideas, questions and favourite bits in their Daily log as they read the text. Explain that it is more important for them to think about what they are reading than to finish first and, as they already know the story, it doesn't matter if they don't finish this time.

evaluate how
authors use
language

Zoom in on sentence types

Purpose: to show how the author uses different sentence types to create imagery

- Tell the children that authors use different types of sentences for all sorts of reasons: to create pace, tone, atmosphere, to make the reader zoom in on details, etc.
- Explain that you are going to zoom in on exactly how Michael Morpurgo varies his sentence types to create imagery and atmosphere.
- Display the extracts from the story on the **CD (file 4.1)**.
- Read each extract and then click 'TOL' to reveal the explanations of what effect each extract creates.
- Display the extract on the final screen (this has no TOL) and ask the children to TTYP to discuss any features of the sentence that they think create imagery or atmosphere. Take feedback.

Drama

Purpose: for children to use drama to explore a central theme in the story

- Explain to the children that you are going to do a whole class improvisation: *The Day they Burnt the Books.*
- Set the scene for the improvisation by reading the description of the book burning from the Anthology p.72 aloud to the children.
- Tell them that they are going to act out this flashback to see how difficult it would be to stand up to an invading army.
- Organise the class into soldiers and townspeople.
- Give the roles of the unicorn lady as a child and her father to two pupils. Tell them that they are going to act out plucking the book out of the fire.
- You are acting in role as the officer and the soldiers will carry out your orders.
- Tell the townspeople that they must obey or they will be punished.
- Start the improvisation by shouting orders to the soldiers so that they form a disciplined line. Order them to round up the townspeople.
- Order the townspeople to get in a line and pass books along towards the fire. Make an imaginary pile of books.
- Start a chant, for example: *Down with books! Books are bad! Burn them! Burn them!* Order the townspeople to join in.

- Once the chant is really going, give the father a signal to pluck a book from the fire. Immediately order the soldiers to seize him! Stop the improvisation here.
- Ask the children to reflect on the improvisation. Direct them to think about how it felt to be ordered or have power or chant and then see the father stand up for himself.

Curriculum link: writing diaries

Daily log

Purpose: for children to empathise with a character by writing in role

- Ask the children to write a diary entry in role as the unicorn lady describing what happened the day her father saved the book *The Little Match Girl*. This piece of writing could be used for part of a scrapbook (see Day 8 Write a story 1).

effective discussion; provide justifications for their views

Big Question (CD)

Purpose: for children to develop their skills of argument and discussion through a mini enquiry session based on a philosophical question relating to the work of the day

- Display today's Big Question on the **CD (file 4.2)**:
  What do you think is worth standing up for?
- Follow the process as explained at the end of Day 1 (p.134).

Who says? A PB

Purpose: for children to develop their awareness of the characters' point of view

discuss viewpoints

- Explain to the children that Michael Morpurgo is exploring the theme of war in this story. Ask the children read the part of the story in the Anthology p.72 where the unicorn lady describes her father saving the book. Tell the children that the author is using this flashback to illustrate how war can make people behave in terrible ways.
- Ask the children to TTYP and discuss what the unicorn lady's point of view about war might be. Take feedback.
- Ask the children to return to the text and read the two paragraphs starting 'Then one summer morning' on p.72. In it are clues to help the children to work out how Tomas, his mother and father feel about war. Model how to work out how Tomas feels about war and then ask them to TTYP and discuss his mother and father's point of view.
- Tell the children to look at Who says? in the Pupils' Book p.53 and TTYP to discuss the different characters' viewpoints. Tell them to use the prompts to help them work out what Michael Morpurgo might feel about war.

consider different accounts of the same event and discuss viewpoints

Daily log: Drama

Purpose: for children to make notes about how a character is feeling

- Take the role of Tomas, or Tomas' father.
- Explain to the children that they will have the chance to hear first hand from one of the characters in the story about what it was like when the army invaded: the day war came to the valley. Ask them to get out their Daily log so they can note down the extra details and information about the invasion whilst the character is talking.
- Tell the children that you are acting in role and explain who you are. You may wish to start with telling the children some details about your character such as your age, job and small details about where you live.
- Now you are going to tell the children, from your character's point of view, what it was like when the army invaded and explain in detail what you saw as you rushed to the town square and saw the library on fire. Below are some details to help you.

- *We hid in the woods and watched the army invade from safety.*
- *We did not know where the unicorn lady was, she may well have been in the library hiding by the unicorn.*
- *The streets in the town had been bombed and windows had been blown out – houses were burning, people were trying to save their belongings.*
- *When we saw the library, the flames and smoke had reached the upper floor windows. It was very difficult to go in and very smoky.*
- *Everyone helped to save the books.*

If you describe what the interior of the library was like, give details and say why you had to stop saving the books, i.e. 'It was boiling and smokey, we couldn't go on any longer'.

Daily log

Purpose: for children to summarise an event in the story

- Ask the children to use the notes they have taken to help them write a newspaper headline and short paragraph to describe the invasion. This piece of writing could be used for part of a scrapbook (see Day 8 Write a story 1).

> **Curriculum link:** developing ideas

What if not...? PB

Purpose: for children to consider how the characters' actions affect the plot

- Ask the children to look at the What if not...? activity in the Pupils' Book p.54. TOL about the first What if not...? question with the children, modelling how the story would change if Tomas held back and refused to join in the storytelling sessions at the library. *He would not have recommended the other older children to come to the sessions, nor would he have rushed to save the books from the fire.*
- Now ask the children to TTYP to discuss the remaining What if not...? questions.

> drawing inferences and justifying with evidence, identifying key details that support ideas

Daily log

Purpose: for children to consider how the characters' actions affect the plot

- Ask the children to record at least one more What if not...? in their Daily log with some notes about how it would affect characters, plot or setting.
  For example: What if not *gone away*? What if *the soldiers came and stayed in the town?* How would this have affected Tomas and his family?

> drawing inferences and justifying with evidence, identifying key details

Big Question CD

Purpose: for children to develop their skills of argument and discussion through a mini enquiry session based on a philosophical question relating to the work of the day

- Display today's Big Question on the **CD (file 5.1)**:

  What is the purpose of war?

- Follow the process as explained at the end of Day 1 (p.134).

> effective discussion; provide justifications for their views

WRITING FICTION

DAY 6

Build a sentence

Purpose: for children to compose sentences that describe a setting

Curriculum link:
understand, through being shown, the skills and processes essential for writing: that is, thinking aloud to generate ideas, drafting, and re-reading to check that the meaning is clear

- Explain that you are going to look at how Michael Morpurgo described the fire at the library. Reveal the passages on the **CD (file 6.1)**. Read aloud and comment on how the author uses the clauses to add more detail. Draw the children's attention to the use of imagery and vivid word choices, such as the *flames licking, smoke billowing* and *faces smudged and blackened.*
- Click 'Sentences' to reveal the words that describe the movement of the flames.
- Re-read sentence 1 using substitutions for *flames licking*. Get feedback from the children about the different choices and comment on their effect on the fierceness of the fire.
- Remind the children how to punctuate a subordinate clause.
- Repeat the activity for sentences 2 and 3.
- Ask the children to TTYP and compose their own version of the final sentence. Take feedback.

Modelled composition

- Tell the children that you are going to compose three sentences that describe the streets after the army has invaded. You are going to use the description of the square by Michael Morpurgo as a basis for your sentence construction.
- Use TOL to explain what you are doing and orally rehearse and change each phrase before writing.
- Ask the children to say each sentence as you compose it using MT/YT and then write it on a flipchart or the board. Continue to use MT/YT as you now TOL and model the writing process. N.B. A script of the writing process can be printed from the **CD (file 6.2)** if you want more support.
- Hide your sentences. Ask the children, either individually or as partners, to compose their own first sentence out loud using the Build a sentence – sentence prompts in their Pupils' Book p.54. Do not let the children write in their Daily log until they can say their sentence out loud.
- Ask partners to take turns to develop each other's sentences. Encourage crossings out, switching words round, etc. Emphasise that this is writing in action – it is not a neat, finished piece of writing!

making comparisons, checking that the story makes sense to them

Tell a story

Purpose: for children to practise oral re-telling of a story

- Show the short text on the **CD (file 6.3)**. Explain that it builds on the sentences from the last activity. It describes the devastation of the town seen through Tomas' eyes and then his feelings as he realises the library could be on fire.
- Read the text to the children.
- Explain that you are going to have a go at re-telling this part of the story to them without looking at the written text. Hide the text. Whilst you are re-telling Tomas' progress down the devastated street ask the children to listen carefully for: 1) missing information; 2) additional information; 3) more everyday language and less description; 4) use of body language, facial expressions and pace and tone to engage the audience.
- Ask the children to TTYP to share what differences they noticed. They may need to refer to the written version of the text in their Pupils' Books p.55 after they have heard the re-telling. Collect feedback.

- Now tell the children that they are going re-read the story using their Pupils' Book p.55. Tell them to take turns to read with expression and intonation to show understanding.
- Next ask the children to continue the story and try to develop the story orally with their partners. Ask them to think about what Tomas sees as he gets to the end of the street and into the square. They should swap roles from teller to listener and vice versa when you say 'swap and stop' at about 30 second intervals (two or three times), continuing the story from that point each time.
- Emphasis should be on building confidence in storytelling and keeping the audience engaged and interested!

Curriculum link: developing ideas

Daily log

Purpose: for children to start to generate ideas for their story

- Ask the children to create a draft of a poster asking the townspeople to look after the library books that have been saved from the fire. This piece of writing could be used for part of a scrapbook (see Day 8 Write a story 1).

effective discussion; provide justifications for their views

Big Question ⓒⒹ

Purpose: for children to develop their skills of argument and discussion through a mini enquiry session based on a philosophical question relating to the work of the day

- Display today's Big Question on the **CD (file 6.4)**:

  If you could only choose one thing what would you save?

- Follow the process as explained at the end of Day 1 (p.134).

DAY 7

Grammar: linking ideas across paragraphs ⓒⒹ 🅿🅱

Purpose: for children to develop their ability to recognise and use a wider range of cohesive devices to link ideas across paragraphs

Year 6 Grammar
linking ideas across paragraphs using a wider range of cohesive devices

- Tell the children that in the story *I Believe in Unicorns* the writer has created lots of layers of meaning through linked images and ideas across times and places. Say that this creates what we call *cohesion* throughout story. Display **CD (file 7.1)** to show a definition of the word and read it aloud to the children.
- Explain that the ideas and images are linked across paragraphs by referring back to what's gone before, to what's happening in the present and what is still to come. Say that there are different ways to create the links through what we call *cohesive* (the adjective form of the noun *cohesion*) *devices*.
- Read through the definition and examples for cohesive devices. Use this as an opportunity to revise the children's understanding of terminology such as *repetition, pronouns* and *adverbials* at the same time.
- Explain that we use most of these cohesive devices automatically, to make our writing flow naturally and to link paragraphs. Tell them it is always a good idea to read through their writing, as they work, to check they have used cohesive devices not just to make their writing clear for the reader, but to enjoy the layers and links in their writing.
- Click 'Next' to show an extract from *I Believe in Unicorns*. Ask the children to read it out chorally with you.
- Click 'Next' to display the extract with highlights to show links between the paragraphs. Click 'TOL' and use the TOL bubble to explain how the images that the writer has created are used as a device to link the paragraphs together.

- Click 'Next' to show the same extract of text with the pronouns highlighted. Click 'TOL' and use the think bubbles to explain how the pronouns are used as a cohesive device.
- Navigate to the next slide and repeat the process, explaining how adverbials and repetition are used to create cohesion.
- Now ask the children to look at the Grammar: linking ideas across paragraphs activity on p.55 of their Pupils' Book. Explain the activity and ask them to complete it with their partners. Make sure they understand that there is not a right answer you are looking for but their own ideas and opinions. Choose different sets of partners to share their ideas and supporting reasons.
- Tell them that another, more tricky cohesive device to use is to let readers make their own links by hinting at something rather than telling the reader directly. Say that you have found a good example of this in the 'Tell a story' text they have read in their Pupils' Book.
- Display **CD (file 7.2)** to show an example from the text to read aloud. Click 'TOL' and use the think bubbles to discuss the implicit links. This is an example of one way of using the grammatical concept of ellision (or ellipsis) as a cohesive device, however, it is possible to explain the device and its effect without using the terminology with the children.

Homework Book p.21 provides further practice on linking ideas across paragraphs.

Curriculum link: describing settings

Build a setting

Purpose: for children to see how a setting can be built up

- Explain that you are going to write a text that slips into Michael Morpurgo's story. You are going to write about Tomas and his father watching the army invade the town in the woods and then travel back into the town once they are sure the army has gone. Then you are going to describe the two of them walking down the deserted streets towards the town square and the library.
- Tell the children that you want to describe the countryside that Tomas and his father walk through to get back to the town and that in this description you want to convey how it has changed, how it has been marked by the army's progress.
- Show the Build a setting prompts on the **CD (file 7.3)**. Explain that you are going to demonstrate how to use our senses to create accurate descriptions of the countryside as it empties of the army and then of the town as Tomas and his father pass through the ruined streets.
- Ask the children to TTYP and discuss the noises that the army, its tanks, planes and weapons might make. Take feedback and write some of the ideas next to the 'Ear' icon. Say that you want to make a contrast between the loud noises of battle and the fading noises of the army.
- Continue using the questions and TTYP to discuss what Tomas will see, smell, feel and hear on his journey. Use the second paragraph of the text in the Pupils' Book pp.56–57 to help you with examples (do not ask the children to look at the questions yet).

plan their writing, understand the processes essential for writing

Plan a story

Purpose: for children to be able to see the planning process of part of a story

- Display Plan a story on the **CD (file 7.4)**. Explain that this is the plan for part of the story from when Tomas and his father watch the army invade from the woods to where they realise the library might be on fire. It has an opening, two incidents and a problem.

- Click 'Reveal' to show the planning and annotations for the opening. Do the same for the other sections of the plan. TOL to model how the annotations in the planning could be used to create ideas for sentences. You could use the completed text in the Pupils' Book p.56 to help you with this.

<table>
<tr><td>

Curriculum link:
using similar writing as models for their own

</td></tr>
</table>

Build an episode

Purpose: for children to see an example of writing that will provide a model for their own writing

- An example story is provided as a model for the children's writing. Explain that the writer has tried to write in a similar style to Michael Morpurgo. Read the episode aloud from the Pupils' Books p.56 with the children following the text.
- Now display the episode on the **CD (file 7.5)**. Review some of the features of Michael Morpurgo's writing, e.g. *layered and connected images* (like the description of the smoke and the references to books being burned), *writing in the first person* and *exploring tricky themes* (like truth and war).
- Using TTYP and oral feedback, ask the children to evaluate the episode using the Guide questions in the Pupils' Book p.57.

preparing poems

Daily log

Purpose: for children to keep a personal reading, writing and thinking log in order to record thoughts and ideas for their own writing

- Tell the children to choose some of the words and images from the story that really described the desolation of the bombed out street. Use them and others to create a non-rhyming poem that captures the atmosphere of the destruction.

effective discussion; provide justifications for their views

Big Question

Purpose: for children to develop their skills of argument and discussion through a mini enquiry session based on a philosophical question relating to the work of the day

- Display today's Big Question on the **CD (file 7.6)**:

  Why should we remember the past?*

- Follow the process as explained at the end of Day 1 (p.134)

* This Big Question will be revisited on Day 11 – the first day of the non-fiction week (p.147)

DAY 8

plan their writing

Write a story 1 📕

Purpose: for children to explore the stimulus and plan the opening of their story

Introduction

- Explain to the children that they are going to write a continuation of Tomas' story, this time about the invaders returning. This story will be supported with other pieces of writing that the children have already done or will do later in this Unit, i.e. artefacts such as the diary entry (Daily log Day 4), the newspaper cutting (Daily log Day 5), and images and posters, which altogether will form their finished extended narrative.
- They can present their finished work as a scrapbook with the story interwoven with their other writing. They will need to think of ways in which to present their work so that the reader can enjoy all the extra pieces of information, as this will make the story seem even more real and interesting.
- They will be using text types that they have practised in their Daily log already and that should be very familiar to them, e.g. they can use the poster asking the townspeople to look after the library books (Daily log Day 6) as a draft for their first artefact in their scrapbooks. They can stick the final piece in their scrapbooks later.

Writing

- Display the images on **CD (file 8.1)**.
- Choose one of the images and give your personal response to it. TOL about how it would feel to be in that picture. Imagine the sounds, smells and sights.
- Ask the children to TTYP and discuss the images that they have seen.
- Tell the children to look at the image in their Pupils' Book p.58 and use the questions to imagine how it would feel to be bombed out of their home. Tell them to make quick notes in their Daily logs. Take feedback.
- Explain that this is the starting point of the next episode of Tomas' story; that his home has been destroyed and he has lost his parents in the confusion. The story will be written through his eyes and will be about how Tomas finds his parents.
- Remind the children of their responses to the image and the questions in the Pupils' Book – these will be the plan for their opening paragraph. Tell the children to review their answers in their Daily logs and change them if they need to so that they reflect Tomas' situation and his point of view.

Curriculum link: discuss viewpoints

Role-play – Lost! ⓒⒹ

Purpose: for children to explore the emotions of their character through role-play

- Ask the children to listen to *Mars, the Bringer of War* by Gustav Holst from *The Planets Suite*. Click on the **CD (file 8.2)**. (The whole piece of music is provided on the file but you may wish to select an extract to play to the children.)
- Ask children to TTYP and discuss the images and emotions that came to them as they listened. Help the children to notice the different moods of the music.
- Tell the children they are going to act in role as Tomas realising that he has lost his parents during the bombing. They are going to use the music to help them act out seeing the bomb-blasted area for the first time and then finding a way out of it. Towards the end of their role-play they have some hope. Perhaps they recognise someone that can help them or they find a clue as to where their parents are.
- Play the music a second time and ask the children to do the role-play described above.
- Give feedback about what you noticed and ask the children to TTYP and discuss how they think Tomas feels by the end of the role-play.
- Ask the children to write short notes in their Daily log.

plan their writing

Write a story 2 ⓒⒹ 🄿🄱 📄

Purpose: for children to plan their story

- Remind the children of the planning that they've done so far in their Daily logs and show them a skeleton of the story plan on the **CD (file 8.3)**. TOL about ideas for the first two sections.
- Ask the children to look at the two final parts of the plan – the incident and the resolution. Discuss the types of things that could happen to Tomas on the way to finding his parents (he could have to run away from soldiers, see someone in trouble and help them, have an accident and be rescued by another character).
- Tell the children to TTYP and discuss their ideas for an incident. Take feedback and scribe some ideas onto the planning skeleton on the **CD (file 8.3)**.
- Now ask the children to TTYP and discuss how their story will be resolved. Ask them to use the Write a story 2 questions in the Pupils' Book p.59 to help them focus the ideas for the final part of the story, i.e. the resolution.
- Take feedback and scribe some more ideas onto the planning skeleton on the **CD (file 8.3)**.
- Print out blank copies of the planning skeleton from the **CD (file 8.4)** for the children to use for their planning.

Curriculum link:
describing setting
and atmosphere

Daily log

Purpose: for children to keep a personal reading, writing and thinking Daily log in order to record thoughts and ideas for their own writing

- Tell the children that they are going to write a draft of a diary entry for their story. It should be from one of Tomas' parents' point of view and tell the story of the bomb hitting their house in the night and losing contact with Tomas. It need only be a fragment of the diary and the writing can be polished later on.

effective
discussion; provide
justifications for
their views

Big Question

Purpose: for children to develop their skills of argument and discussion through a mini enquiry session based on a philosophical question relating to the work of the day

- Display today's Big Question on the **CD (file 8.5)**:

  Who suffers most during a war?

- Follow the process as explained at the end of Day 1 (p.134).

Write a story 3

writing narratives

Purpose: for children to write their episode about the second invasion and Tomas' search for his parents.

- *N.B. By the end of this session the children now have drafts in their Daily log of a diary entry, poster, poem and newspaper clipping. They will need additional time to finish these and research any pictures that they want to include in their finished story scrapbook.*
- Tell the children that they are ready to write their own episode about the second invasion and Tomas' search for his parents. Remind them that they have detailed plans on the planning skeleton that set out the structure of their episode and create the linking themes and imagery for the story.
- Ask them to use the Write a story 3 writing checklist in the Pupils' Book p.59 to guide them. Tell them to use any useful parts of their Daily log to help them.
- Remind them to look at the Word wall for Power words and phrases as well as to consider how to link images by using powerful accurate vocabulary. Remind them that they looked at how to link ideas across paragraphs earlier in the Unit and that they should try to include such links.
- Encourage children to rehearse their opening sentence with their partners before they begin to write.
- You may wish to display the sentences you modelled with the children and/or the developed paragraph on the **CD (file 6.3)**.

Share a story

Purpose: for children to read and share their story

- Ask the children to read through their own episode.
- Now tell them to re-read their episode and underline their favourite or best parts. Ask them to share these with their partners. Collect feedback on best bits from partners.
- Make sure that any powerful words or phrases are written on card and added to the Word wall.

assessing the
effectiveness of
their own and
others' writing

Evaluate and edit (CD)

Purpose: for children to evaluate their own and their partner's work against specific criteria and then discuss how they could improve their work

- Display **CD (file 10.1)** to show the evaluation prompts and read them together using MT/YT.
- As a model, select an example of work from the children where the writing has met the criteria, and share this with the other children, explaining why it works well.
- Tell the children to take turns to read their partner's writing and discuss how well they have met the criteria.
- Ask children to discuss at least two changes they could make to improve their work following the partner discussion.

Curriculum link: proofread for spelling and punctuation errors

Proofread

Purpose: for children to proofread their work and make changes to improve the accuracy of their grammar, punctuation and spelling

- Now ask the children to proofread their work. If you have noticed that several children need to improve on a particular aspect of spelling, grammar or punctuation, use this as a focus for the Proofread activity. Write an example which includes common errors from the children's writing and use this as a model.
- The children should always be checking for standard use of punctuation and correct spelling of common exception words.
- The following points would be relevant as the particular focus for this Unit:
  - check for consistent use of the first person and past tense
  - check that speech is punctuated correctly
  - check that common verbs haven't been overused, e.g. run, scared, looked.

effective discussion; provide justifications for their views, distinguish between fact and opinion

Very Big Question

Purpose: for children to explore one of the Big Questions in more depth

- See Unit 1 Day 10 for teaching notes on the Very Big Question p.36.

Explanations

READING AND WRITING NON-FICTION

In the non-fiction part of the Unit children examine the explanation text 'How does a story become a Manga graphic novel?' and write their own explanation text on a book-based theme using a range of Internet sources.

See p.130 for the daily timetable for the Non-fiction week.

Non-fiction

Reading

Children will:

- distinguish explanations from instructions
- understand the key features of explanations and identify them in texts
- research authors' websites and discuss how different features have been used.

Writing

Key writing purpose to be shared with the children:

To write a text explaining how to make a book a best-seller, focusing in particular on how authors can engage readers through websites.

Writing evaluation to be shared with the children

My explanation text:

- includes key points gathered from my research
- is organised so that it is clear and engaging for the reader
- uses features of explanation texts where relevant, e.g. *headings, labelled pictures, questions to engage the reader.*

Grammar:

- includes causal language and adverbials of time to structure information for the reader.

See the Planning section of the Software ('Timetables' tab) for a printable version of the Writing purpose and evaluation.

DAY 11

Curriculum link: learn the conventions of different types of writing

Linking the texts (CD)

Purpose: for children to make links between the story text and the non-fiction text

- Display the Big Question from Day 7 on the **CD (file 7.6)** *Why should we remember the past?*
- Remind the children of the ideas that they came up with when discussing this question.
- Draw their attention to the word *why* and say that when a question begins with the word *why* or *how* it usually needs an explanation as an answer. TOL explaining a couple of the reasons for people talking about the past such as: 'We *talk about the past in order that we can remember how bad war is so we don't go to war again unless it is really necessary.*' (Causal language.)
- Ask the children to TTYP to think of an explanation why we should remember the past and take feedback.
- Explain to the children that explanations tell us how or why something happens. These texts help us understand events or give us more information about how something works or why something occurs. They are not instructions but they may well help us do something.

---

making comparisons

Introduction PB (CD)

Purpose: for children to understand the context for the study of the non-fiction explanation text

- Remind the children about the story that they have been studying. Tell them that you have discovered two artefacts from the invasion which tell the people in Tomas' town what to do in case of an invasion (a set of instructions and an explanation).
- Ask them to take turns to read each section of the two 'Invasion!' texts in the Pupils' Book pp.60–61.
- Use TOL to compare and contrast the texts, focusing on the text types, the purpose of the texts, the layout and the language used. Use the chart on the **CD (file 11.1)** to help organise your comparison.
- Ask the children to TTYP and discuss which of the texts they feel would be more useful if they were invaded.

---

learn the conventions of different types of writing

Instructions and explanations (CD)

Purpose: for children to distinguish between instructions and explanations

- Tell the children that both the texts tell the reader what to do. The instructional text has less detail and gives sequential orders, whereas the explanation tells the reader how, why, where and what to do and is not just a series of commands.
- Explain that these two texts have different features: the instructional text uses the imperative verb (*listen* and *take*) and adverbials of time (*Once*), whereas the explanation uses the present tense and has adverbials of time (*when, finally, until*) and causal language (*although, which*).
- Display the special phrases sorting game on the **CD (file 11.2)**.
- Use TOL to discuss the first two phrases and drag them on to the causal language or adverbials of time circle.
- Then ask the children to TTYP to discuss the rest of the phrases. Take feedback and move each phrase to the correct place.

---

identifying the audience for the writing

Audience PB

Purpose: for children to evaluate the purpose of a text

- Ask the children to return to the 'Invasion!' texts in the Pupils' Book pp.60–61 and read them silently.

- Use TOL to compare the purpose of the two invasion texts thinking about where and when you might see them. Review the fact that the explanation gave more detail so that the reader could understand why, how and where you would be evacuated to. But the instructions were brief and could be remembered much more easily.
- Ask the children to TTYP and discuss when each of the texts would be most useful and where or in what form they might be found (posters, leaflets, radio broadcast, newspaper advert, etc.).

Curriculum link: noting ideas, drawing on research

Daily log

Purpose: for children to keep a personal reading, writing and thinking log in order to record thoughts and ideas for their own writing

- Tell the children that over the next few days you want them to look in magazines, newspapers, on the Internet or packaging for examples of explanation writing of any kind. Ask them to bring them to school to stick them in their Daily log. Tell them to write a note next to each one explaining where they found it. Tell them to make sure they are not all from the Internet!

DAY 12

using similar writing as models for their own

Deconstruction 1

Purpose: for children to see an example of writing that will provide a model for the planning of their own writing

- Ask the children to find 'How does a story become a Manga graphic novel?' in their Anthology p.77. Ask them to take turns to read a section of the explanation aloud using expression and intonation to show understanding.
- Display an excerpt of the text on the **CD (file 12.1)** and draw the children to the key features of an explanation by highlighting:
  - a general statement as an introduction to the topic (*A graphic novel, on the other hand,…*)
  - technical language (*Manga, illustrations*)
  - adverbials of time and causal language (*nowadays, on the other hand*)
  - the complex sentences which give extra information.
- Explain that this text will be used as a reference to help them to plan their own explanation, which will be: *How to make your book a best-seller.*
- Ask them to return to the graphic novel text in the Anthology and TTYP to share whether the explanation gives clear information about: 1) What a graphic novel is 2) Who is involved in creating a graphic novel 3) How the text is converted into the graphic novel 4) How action, emotion and split locations are shown in a graphic novel. Take feedback.
- Now return to the text in the Anthology to point out additional organisational features, such as the introduction, the short factual sentences, pictures with captions, etc.

identifying key details

Read an explanation

Purpose: for children to understand and locate examples of the key features of an explanation text

- Display the key features checklist grid on the **CD (file 12.2)** and click on the 'Complete' icon to show the examples. TOL to explain the completed examples.
- Print out one between two copies of the empty grid from the **CD (file 12.3)**. Tell the children to work with their partners to complete their own grids using the complete text from the Anthology pp.77–80 about creating a graphic novel. Take feedback.

Curriculum link: noting ideas

Daily log

Purpose: for children to keep a personal reading, writing and thinking log in order to record thoughts and ideas for their own writing

- Ask the children to find examples of Manga or Graphic novels and make notes about how the action is portrayed.

DAY 13

summarising the main ideas

Deconstruction 2

Purpose: for children to break down the key ideas for their explanation

- Tell the children that they are going to write an explanation that helps an author make their book a best-seller. Explain that writing a great story isn't enough to make your book a best-seller. Authors have to do publicity events, have a website and find ways of telling as many people as possible about themselves and their book in order to sell lots of copies!
- Show the children Michael Morpurgo's website http://www.michaelmorpurgo.com/ and click on *Events*. Read aloud some of the events that he will be taking part in. Ask the children to TTYP and discuss the types of events he is a part of. Take feedback.
- Display the mind map on the **CD (file 13.1)** and use the ideas captured by the children about author events under the heading *Events*.
- Now return to the website and click the link *About Michael Morpurgo*. Skim through the page noting how there is some personal information, photos and questions and answers.
- Ask the children to TTYP and discuss what information is on the *About* section of the website. Take feedback and add this information under *Website, Reviews and Interviews* on the mind map.
- Now visit the Jeremy Strong website http://www.jeremystrong.co.uk/ and look at the links on the top of the page. Click on the 'About Me'. Ask the children to TTYP and see how many ways you could contact Jeremy Strong. Take feedback.
- Return to the mind map and add this information under the heading *Personal contact*.

retrieve, record and present information from non-fiction

Build an explanation – plan

Purpose: for children to make a plan for their explanation using a range of Internet sources

> *N.B. This activity would work best if the children had access to the Internet and could navigate to various author websites.*

- Print off your annotated mind map from the **CD (file 13.1)** and give a copy to each child so that they can take notes and make the initial plan for their explanation.
- Tell the children that they are going to have a quick information collection session to add ideas to the mind map (ideally 15 minutes). You may want to print a copy of the blank mind map from the **CD (file 13.2)** for children to add their ideas to. Direct them to the Top Tips for taking notes in the Pupils' Book p.62 and ask them to TTYP and take turns to read the advice aloud to each other. Take feedback.
- Show them the heading *My ideas* where they can add their own or researched ideas about how to promote a book. These could be ideas they gather from the other author websites they visit.
- Below is a list of children's author websites that show a range of ideas and events that authors do to promote their books.

Neil Gaiman	http://www.mousecircus.com/ (child friendly site)
Anne Fine	http://www.annefine.co.uk/
Julia Golding	http://www.juliagolding.co.uk/
Marcus Sedgwick	http://www.marcussedgwick.com/
Quentin Blake	http://www.quentinblake.com/

- Once the children have gathered an adequate amount of information take feedback for each of the areas of the mind map.
- Now model how to refine the mind map into a more coherent plan for the explanation by pruning similar ideas/words and bringing some ideas together in more cohesive phrases. For example, events could be refined to book launches, festivals, school visits. Which then could be brought together as: *Authors get publicity by doing events like festivals and book launches. School visits are good opportunities for authors to meet their fans.*

> **Curriculum link:**
> identifying key details

Daily log

Purpose: for children to refine their mind maps into notes

- Ask the children stick their mind maps into their Daily log and to refine their notes, pruning away extra detail and bringing together ideas.

Deconstruction 3 **PB**

> developing initial ideas

Purpose: for children to see an example of writing that will provide an opportunity for them to evaluate the effectiveness of layout, organisation and clarity

- Tell the children to read the 'How to find a book in the library' text in the Pupils' Book pp.63–64. Then ask them to scan the text looking at how the writer has helped the reader and to find the organisational features listed on p.64.
- Tell the children that they need to choose organisational features that order their explanation logically so that the reader has the best chance of understanding what they are trying to say. Images and diagrams will really help the reader understand more complicated ideas. Using an image like a screenshot or a mock up of a website might really help part of their explanation.
- Ask the children to TTYP and discuss which of these organisational features would be good to have in their explanation. Take feedback.

Write an explanation ⓒⒹ **PB** **A**

Purpose: for children to use their planning and notes to help them to write an explanation text

- Display the section of the mind map and notes on the **CD (file 14.1)**.
- Now use TOL to show how you would develop the notes into a short text explaining about how to make an author website brilliant.
- TOL: 'I want to give this a fun heading and I want it to be a question – that will help to keep me focused as I write.' What makes a really brilliant author website?
- 'My first sentence will introduce the main idea.' Authors need websites to connect with their fans and the people who might become their fans.

'Next I'm going to ask a question that I will answer straight away.'

So what makes a website really good? Well a good website has up-to-date information about the author, but a great website does so much more! It makes the reader feel like they really can get to know the author, about their ideas and about their books.

'The next sentences will use the information from my notes and I will make causal links saying why these website features are a great idea so that the reader will know why they would like to have those things on their author website.'

- Tell the children to read the rest of the explanation in the Pupils' Books p.64. Point out the causal language (*which, Although*) and the adverbial of time (*In recent years*).
- Tell the children that they are ready to write their explanation of How to make your book a best-seller. Remind them that they need to think of an introduction that tells the reader about how simply writing a great book isn't enough. That behind every best-seller lots of work goes on and you are going to explain how this works.